PRAISE FOR *KEEP GOING: A GUIDE TO ORGANIZING WHEN IT'S HARD*

"Against the seemingly limitless power of corporations and billionaires, and the cruelty of a government turning against its own people, there are workers everywhere standing up and fighting back. I've known Ellen David Friedman for many years. She knows what it takes to organize and give people real hope. This book contains that experience and helps anyone who is building power in the workplace—step by step, facing endless challenges—to keep going."

—SENATOR BERNIE SANDERS

"Each page will help you gain and build momentum when you feel stuck. It's easy to get frustrated, to complain or take a step back. But this book equips you to lean into problems and push through, keeping an eye on the horizon. Every real-world story delivers an organizing principle that will help you build collective power with your colleagues and create a democratic union along the way."

—JON SCHLEUSS, President, The NewsGuild-CWA

"*Keep Going* captures the need for humility in organizing, especially when things get hard. Through storytelling, Ellen shares organizing lessons that respond to common organizing questions and challenges, and that provoke thought about the processes of organizing often taken for granted or forgotten."

—DIAMONTÉ BROWN, President, Baltimore Teachers Union

"In this era of oligarchy, workers are up against great odds, and their best hope lies in their ability to organize. Ellen David Friedman's book faces the harsh challenges of organizing, and offers not only concrete guidance but also examples of success. It is based on real experience and provides wonderful guidance."

—LARRY COHEN, President (2005-2015), Communications Workers of America

"Unions are more admired than they have been in a half century. Maybe it's because of people like Ellen David Friedman, who are rebuilding unions that are democratic, led by rank-and-file members, and fearlessly committed to winning what workers need. That vision, lost in too many unions, is irresistible—to workers inside unions, and to those not yet organized. Ellen was advising us from the start of our decade-long transformation of the Massachusetts Teachers Association into a fighting union. If your union is breaking your heart, or you are at the start of building the union you deserve, or like all of us, you're figuring out how to overcome the latest outrage by your boss, read this book and you'll gain new inspiration to *Keep Going*."

—MAX PAGE, President, Massachusetts Teachers Association

"While many organizing books focus narrowly on techniques, *Keep Going* hits on key fundamentals, putting questions of union democracy and power front and center. It combines practical advice with fundamental insights on organizing."

—JOE BURNS, labor attorney/negotiator and author of *Class Struggle Unionism*

KEEP GOING

A GUIDE TO ORGANIZING WHEN IT'S HARD

ELLEN DAVID FRIEDMAN

PMPRESS

A LABOR NOTES BOOK

Keep Going: A Guide to Organizing When It's Hard

Reprints

ISBN: 979-8-88744-099-6 (paperback)
ISBN: 979-8-88744-205-1 (ebook)
Library of Congress Control Number: 2026933419

Cover design by John Yates / stealworks.com
Cover illustration by Fernando Martí
Illustrations by Fernando Martí
Interior design by Sonia Singh

10 9 8 7 6 5 4 3 2 1

Labor Notes
55 Washington St Suite 522
Brooklyn, NY 11201

PM Press
PO Box 23912
Oakland, CA 94623
www.pmpress.org

Printed in Canada

For my family
and
my family of comrades

CONTENTS

ACKNOWLEDGMENTS

Many hands helped assemble this book.

Dan DiMaggio hatched the idea to collect Ellen's popular how-to articles from *Labor Notes* into a book, and he conducted and transcribed hours of interviews with Ellen, generating additional material. Dan, Jane Slaughter, and Alexandra Bradbury sifted through these transcripts to distill the gems that would become *Keep Going*.

Alexandra worked closely with Ellen to organize the distilled material into an outline and then to edit it into a complete manuscript, along the way incorporating perceptive feedback and ideas from Dan and Jane, as well as from Keith Brower Brown, Jenny Brown, Jack Davies, Joe DeManuelle-Hall, Luis Feliz Leon, Sarah Hughes, Tenaya Lafore, Kevin Lin, Barbara Madeloni, José Roque Pérez-Zetune, Courtney Smith, and Lisa Xu.

Laura McClure's sharp copy editing brought the manuscript over the finish line.

Amy Calandrella, Scott Houldieson, Kai Ortiz-Sugimoto, Yolanda Peoples, Carlos Perez, Antonio Rosario, Basia Sokal, and Kate Ziegler generously shared stories from their own experiences, featured at the beginnings of chapters 1–8.

The book includes excerpts of *Labor Notes* articles by Joe Fahey and Barbara Madeloni, and of the book *Democracy Is Power* by Martha Gruelle and Mike Parker.

Fernando Martí created the gorgeous illustrations. Sonia Singh did the interior design and layout. John Yates designed the cover, featuring one of Fernando's illustrations. Chris Dodge did the index (and proofreading).

Ramsey Kanaan at PM Press provided invaluable advice on many aspects of book production, and proposed co-publishing.

The book is printed by union workers at Marquis in Montmagny, Québec, Canada.

PREFACE: BECOMING AN ORGANIZER

When I was 15, I read Jonathan Kozol's book *Death at an Early Age*. It was 1967, and I had already begun to see the cracks in an "American dream" that promised equality, opportunity, and democracy. But what I learned from Kozol about the brutalities of public education for Black students in Boston cracked open my heart and mind.

I asked my parents to front me cash to buy a case of Kozol's book. Then I spent the summer going door to door in my neighborhood to share my revelations and sell copies. I was on fire.

In retrospect, I wonder what my neighbors must have thought. My neighborhood was a modest postwar suburb, all white, nearly all Jewish, and far removed from the horrors Kozol described. But I sold the books. I saw that I was a good talker. And I saw that ideas and words had power.

I was moved by the hard fact of unfairness, and I wanted to *do something* about it. I wanted people to consider Kozol's ideas for themselves, and I wanted us to take action. Because I was starting to see that there must be an "us," not just a "me," if we were to fix things.

I was becoming an organizer—though I didn't know it yet.

Around that same time, the United Farm Workers was ramping up a national boycott of California grapes, an audacious and unprecedented campaign to get growers to recognize the union. UFW leader Dolores Huerta came to speak near my neighborhood, looking for volunteers. She believed that anyone—even a white suburban kid like me—could do something to help win this righteous fight.

I was starting to see that there must be an "us," not just a "me," if we were to fix things.

I was hooked. Weekend after weekend I stood in front of the local Gristedes Supermarket, handing out leaflets, explaining the boycott to housewives, and asking them to honor the lives of Mexican farmworkers 3,000 miles away by not buying grapes.

Such "cold conversations" make a lot of new organizers skittish, but I was motivated enough to vault over my own fears. I loved the idea that we can discuss injustices with strangers, and that this can lead to real, positive change. And the more I organized, the easier it got.

Ever since then, the through line in my life has been organizing, especially with workers fighting exploitation.

When I was in college, I picketed with striking waitresses at a local muffin shop. But then I saw that the support they really needed from me was babysitting for their kids—which I attempted, awkwardly, to provide. This was when I realized that "solidarity" meant offering what workers needed, not what I imagined they needed.

In the early 1970s, I moved to Vermont, where I met Bernie Sanders. I worked with and for him for decades, building the Vermont Progressive Party along the way.

Bernie's success showed me that it is possible to be "radical," to criticize bosses and even capitalism itself, and still win over people we might call "conservative." As he often said, we don't have to agree on everything, but if we agree on something, we can do something.

But trying to elect politicians to office—even those with Bernie's integrity—always felt inadequate to me. I was convinced that challenging the status quo required direct action by workers. We had to harness the productivity and intelligence that workers were otherwise turning over to their bosses every day.

I decided that I wanted to be a labor organizer.

To learn the trade, I drove through the back hills of Vermont and ferreted out experienced old communists and trade unionists. Many were retired members of the United Electrical Workers who had worked in Vermont's once-thriving machine tool industry. I sat for hours in cramped kitchens, drinking instant coffee and soaking in every bit of wisdom I could.

In the early 1980s, I was part of a drive to organize workers producing aviation equipment at a General

Electric plant in Rutland. Unfortunately, workers weren't convinced that they needed "outside" help, and the drive ultimately failed. Clearly, workers needed to begin seeing themselves as the union. But I didn't yet know how I could contribute to such a transformation.

I learned another lesson at a staff job with the American Federation of State, County, and Municipal Employees. One day I went to meet the president of a school custodians union in Montpelier, Vermont's tiny capital city. The building secretary directed me to the basement utility room, but it was vacant. It turned out that the entire custodial staff had trooped off—in a spontaneous work action—to the superintendent's office to challenge a unilateral schedule change.

By the time I caught up with them, the custodians had already forced the superintendent to bargain and, satisfied with the resolution, walked back to school. My presence was barely noticed. Direct collective action got the goods.

By the mid-1980s I was obsessed with democracy and its enemies. The anti-democratic features of capitalism—the concentration of wealth and power—were accelerating everywhere. Even in our unions, elected officers were starting to look and behave like CEOs—permanently off the job, pulling high salaries and personal expense accounts, controlling the resources and decisions, and treating members like customers.

Horrified, I wanted to buttress the most decentralized, bottom-up union I could find… and landed at the Vermont branch of the National Education Association. There I remained for two decades, organizing school support staff and teachers.

I worked on innumerable campaigns, issue fights, elections, strikes, and community coalitions, always looking for ways to include the ideas and contributions of members. I learned to stop promising guaranteed results. Instead, I conveyed that something can always be done, if we connect at the worksite level and build up from there. This approach got so many members involved in bargaining, grievances, and organizing that our membership rate rose to above 90 percent.

Over time I saw that it's not enough to have union leaders who want to fight the boss from the top down. If you bring members a campaign plan that has been beautifully designed by officers or staff, you might get compliant participation, even enthusiasm, and possibly gratitude that someone has "done all this work." But this doesn't leave the members feeling more powerful.

For that, you need to spark members' critical intelligence and inspire their commitment to beating the bastards who are beating us. That requires a bottom-up, deeply democratic organizing process.

The real goal is to enable as many members as possible to become organizers. Achieving this may require us to change long-held practices in our unions—because turning members into organizers often doesn't go down well with officers or staff.

Helping others see and know themselves as organizers has been the task of my "retirement" years. (I put that in quotes because I have been judged a failure at retirement, and I plead guilty.)

The real goal is to enable as many members as possible to become organizers.

Becoming an organizer is not about mastering a formula or a set of predetermined steps. It's certainly not about making a certain number of "asks" per contact, or closing a deal, or selling the union, or getting your co-workers to do what you want them to do. Compliance is what the boss demands. Our organizing should be the opposite: an invitation.

Organizing is not a demand, but an invitation.

I have worked closely with thousands of union members, staffers, and officers over the last half century, applying these approaches to help them organize. There's always a big sigh of relief when I encourage someone to let go of the urgent need to produce a win, meet a metric, or get people to do a certain thing—and instead to focus on building relationships, based on shared goals that are strong enough for us to take risks together.

I've worked in the small world of Vermont for decades, but I also lived in Guangzhou, China, for 10 years and worked at many levels of the Chinese labor movement, until I was expelled by National Security Police in 2015.

In China, the limits and consequences of organizing under an authoritarian government were never far away. Though short-term strikes were tolerated—for back pay, better food in the cafeteria, or to fix dangerous conditions—repression would be swift if workers linked up and tried to form an independent union or democratize their branch of the one legally recognized union, the state-controlled All-China Federation of Trade Unions.

As long as the militancy was limited to brief acts of defiance and not translated into stable organizations, workers couldn't sustain any wins. I learned what the real goal always must be: building relationships that can withstand repression, and whenever possible, securing them through some form of organization.

I've always been connected to a wider labor movement through the portal of Labor Notes, the media and education project that has championed bottom-up, democratic, militant unionism since the late 1970s. With this constant source of grounding and inspiration, I've come to understand that any labor struggle, in any workplace, in any sector, can strengthen our collective long-term work to challenge inequality and exploitation.

The key, I believe, is the presence of many workers who understand that organizing is a long haul, and who resolve to keep going—and to keep each other going.

INTRODUCTION: HOW TO USE THIS BOOK

This book is a companion for workplace organizers. It's a guide to help you get started, help you keep going, and help you get unstuck when you feel mired in the mud or things aren't going the way you envisioned them.

Maybe your situation feels impossible to you right now. Maybe it feels like with all the obstacles in your particular workplace, there's no way to bring people together, no demand you can win. But my experience tells me that's not true. There's always something you can do, even if you have to start with something very small. This book will help you figure out what that something is.

Organizing is full of challenges and dilemmas. How do you decide who to talk to, if your co-workers all seem scared or just apathetic? What if you invite people to a meeting and no one comes? What should you do when your organizing committee is splitting apart? This book will help you to evaluate each situation and find a way forward.

When you set out to organize, you're fighting on a terrain that the boss controls. Up against their power and resources, and a culture that they have shaped, what do we workers have? We have the ability to form relationships with each other—to respect each other, which the boss doesn't—and to think for ourselves. Collectively, we have tremendous potential power: the power to withhold our labor, which makes the world go round. As the song says, "Without our brains and muscles not a single wheel can turn." But without building relationships with our co-workers, we can't access this power.

Organizing is ongoing. It's a way of being and a set of attitudes and values you carry with you every day. The more you bring organizing values into everything you do, the stronger your group will get. The more democratic your approach, the better you and your co-workers can navigate around obstacles, keep going when you're demoralized or overwhelmed, and even learn from defeats.

WHAT'S IN THIS BOOK, AND WHAT ISN'T

This book does not primarily focus on the mechanics of organizing ("get an employee list, map the departments, find the natural leaders"). These methods are essential—and you can read about them in another Labor Notes book, *Secrets of a Successful Organizer*—though you'll have to adapt them to your own situation.

Instead, this book is meant to help you and your fellow organizers develop a rock-solid foundation—an analysis and a set of values you can rely on as you navigate a way forward. Here's how it's structured:

Part I: Four Principles for Organizers

The first part of the book describes some essential principles for organizers to live by, with a chapter for each:

- Cultivate respect.
- Organize democratically.
- Stay grounded in reality.
- Stay steady.

Part II: Ingredients of Successful Organizing

In my experience, organizing boils down to a few recognizable ingredients—whether you're trying to organize a new union, improve one that isn't functioning very well, or organize a contract campaign, strike, or election. Part II has one chapter for each ingredient:

- Help your co-workers understand power in the workplace.
- Overcome division and come together around common concerns.
- Overcome fear and take collective action.
- Reflect on the changing balance of power and keep going.

The order is flexible—you might apply two of these steps at once, or backtrack to repeat them. Use them to orient yourself: *Where am I now, and what am I doing as an organizer?* Also use them to communicate with others around you: *What are we trying to achieve?*

Part III: Getting Unstuck

As soon as you start trying to organize, you start running into roadblocks. Now what?

Part III provides guidance on how you might apply the principles and ingredients of organizing in common situations: *How to get unstuck in case of...* If you're coming to this book with a certain problem on your mind, feel free to browse the table of contents and flip straight to the topic that speaks to you.

You'll start to see how you can use these ideas to get yourself unstuck, no matter what situation you're in.

Part IV: Think Again...

Part IV covers some common organizing practices you may have learned, and proposes that you rethink them.

Are you "selling" the union, but finding that your co-workers aren't buying? Do you notice that your passion and indignation aren't lighting a fire under others? What if you ran for office expecting to transform your union, but you've been disappointed in the results?

If you've asked yourself *Why isn't this working?* you might find answers here.

WHEN YOUR UNION BREAKS YOUR HEART

Perhaps you've found your way to this book because your own union leaders have broken your heart. You tried to get active in the union, but leaders didn't welcome you. Or you brought up a serious issue and were told "there's nothing we can do." Or you and your co-workers worked long and hard on a big campaign, only to be undercut or straight-up sold out.

When this happens, it can feel pretty harsh. But disappointments can be the spur to build a better union.

When Chicago teachers realized their union leaders wouldn't fight school closures, and when auto workers learned their national officers were accepting bribes from the bosses, some members didn't give up. Instead, they transformed their unions from the bottom up and turned them into two of the most powerful and inspiring unions in the U.S.

There's one surefire way to heal your broken heart: Help your co-workers to become organizers too.

MORE TALK, MORE ACTION

Throughout this book, you'll find that conversations are the building block of organizing. That's how you get more people involved over time. And it's how you and your co-workers figure out how to handle any particular situation—by talking it through. Your main insights will come from listening to each other and helping each other to interpret your experiences.

So one of the first things any organizer needs to do is find some buddies. Organizing is not a solo pursuit. Maybe at first it's just one or two other people in your workplace who are interested in making a change. (Maybe you can read this book together!) You'll know your organizing is making headway as the group of people you're talking with starts to grow, and the circle widens.

On nearly every page, you'll be encouraged to have more conversations. Bring people together to talk; fan out and talk to others about what you discussed; come back together to talk about how that went; and so on.

But make no mistake—the goal of all these conversations is *action*. We're not just out to make new friends or generate good vibes at work, though those are pleasant side effects. The point is to shift power.

MAKE MORE ORGANIZERS

In the long run, helping other people become organizers has a lot more impact than just getting them to do something, no matter how urgent that "something" may be.

Multiplying the number of organizers is the best way to sustain yourself in the movement, build power, and improve the culture in a broken union. You don't need permission from anyone, you don't need a budget or union resources, you don't need to be "in the know" or a labor expert... you can simply decide that this is your priority.

Nurturing your co-workers to become organizers is not beyond the capacity of anyone reading this book. (And by actively applying the principles and strategies offered here, you can also become a more confident and effective organizer yourself.)

Bring others with you. Talk about what you see, how you understand the situation, what you are trying to accomplish—and ask what they see, how they understand the situation, what they're trying to accomplish.

The job is to do this work together with co-workers, without too much ego or need to be in charge. Treat people as equals and invite them in.

FIND THE SMALL VICTORIES

How do you know your organizing is bearing fruit? Major victories like contract gains, powerful strikes, or election wins may be few and far between. They're usually the culmination of years-long campaigns made up of a great many small successes (and setbacks) along the way.

So one goal of this book is to help you identify the day-to-day victories that show you're on the right track. Each chapter begins with a success story, and those successes run the gamut from big to small. Inevitably these wins were followed by more twists and turns. Rarely is any victory—or any defeat—the true end of the story.

That's why, as you go along, you have to take satisfaction in every little sign of progress, and avoid overreacting to every loss or misstep. Take notice when you see a lightbulb go on for one person, or when more people sign this petition than the last one, or when your group takes a new risk together. Even if the outcome isn't what you had hoped for, it all adds up. Keep going.

PART I: FOUR PRINCIPLES FOR ORGANIZERS

Begin with the idea that your co-workers have dignity and deserve a say in their own lives, and you'll start to see the path to building collective power.

The following chapters describe four fundamental principles for organizers to live by. These principles will help you to find the path (or find your way back to it) in all kinds of weather. The principles are:

- Cultivate respect
- Organize democratically
- Stay grounded in reality
- Stay steady

CHAPTER 1: CULTIVATE RESPECT

ccR
LOW EMISSION
PSE

The Elevator and the Barbecue

Amy Calandrella learned the first building block of organizing—how to talk to her fellow workers—as an apprentice operating engineer on a construction site where her job was running the elevator, carrying supplies and workers from different trades up and down between floors.

It wasn't easy. "I was a brand new construction worker with a billion sweaty men in a tiny stainless steel box," she said. The door would open, someone would step in, and she would have 45 seconds with that person. Repeat over and over.

To make the days tolerable, "I had to figure out how to get them to talk to me about things that were interesting, as opposed to whatever they were most upset about at the moment," she said. "You're a stressed and upset worker, you're going to want to talk. How can I change the channel and get you to talk about something that isn't horrible for me and also might make this more pleasant for you? Because how much can you really repeat how upset you are at your boss or your ex-wife and still have a pleasant day?"

She started figuring out what people's "benign interests" were. "I would ask a question like, 'How long have you been in the union?' or 'What do you really love about being an electrician?' Sometimes I would just point at a tool and ask what it did. You can draw the teacher out of people.

"Sometimes I would ask for their love story. They would want to blurt it all out, and I would say 'No, tell me chapter 1, and you're going to have to go down eventually and then you can tell me chapter 2.' I had like 45 different conversations going at once with 45 different guys, and that's what I did all day long."

There were also long waits when no one was using the elevator. To stave off boredom, Calandrella put up a map of the world, and this too became a conversation-starter. People would tell her their immigration stories, pointing out where their grandmother or they themselves had come from. As a worker you can start to feel like "your entire world is your ability to put up drywall," she said. The visual reminder of a wider world "did something to people's minds."

"You have to show someone you're interested in them."

Through all these conversations, "I learned how to have a rapport with all kinds of people," Calandrella said, "and I built a muscle for how to steer a conversation without manhandling it too much. I started asking, 'Do you have any girls in your union?' and they would give me women's numbers. I started texting all these women I'd never met before." By the end of the job, she says, "I got the phone number for every female construction worker in western Massachusetts."

Starting from these contacts, Calandrella and others have built a local organization of women in the building trades. They do tabling at career fairs and hold social events to build relationships across the trades. "I try to teach organizing skills through barbecue planning," she says. "I teach people it's possible to have relationships with people you don't already know, or necessarily like. You can just call somebody and say, 'Hey I saw you a couple weeks ago, my name is Amy, we're organizing this barbecue, we'd love for you to…' You have to show someone you're interested in them."

Also, "you have to ask them to bring something. If you don't, they won't come." The women in the group are tough, the do-it-myself type, Calandrella says. So when they're organizing a barbecue for 60 people, "they're like, 'We're going to bring the whole barbecue between the five of us.'" But she tells them, "No, you're not allowed to bring the paper towels! You have to call so-and-so and ask her to do it."

Bringing the paper towels is a simple task anyone can do, but it's not makework—it's really needed. And contributing to something, even in a small way, changes your relationship to it: This barbecue is partly yours now. The woman who brought the paper towels may start thinking up ideas for the next event, and what role she'd like to play. Meanwhile the woman who asked her has practiced a habit she can carry over into her union work—resisting the urge to volunteer herself to write every grievance, lead every meeting, circulate every petition, paint all the signs, order all the pizzas, and speak at every rally.

Sometimes would-be organizers are nervous about bothering people. "You're not bothering somebody when you ask them to participate," Calandrella says. "You're giving them an opportunity to be of use and to feel like they are important, they matter. They're just hanging out wondering if they matter or not. That's what everyone does. So if you call them they're gonna be like, 'My God, someone knows I exist! Yeah, of course I'll bring the plastic cutlery.'"

Solidarity among co-workers is the only possible source of power against the employer. And one essential ingredient for solidarity is respect.

In the workplace we typically don't experience respect—we experience coercion. No matter how much the boss may call us "partners" or claim "we're a family here," the employment relationship is fundamentally undemocratic: The employer makes the decisions, and workers are required to comply.

The union must be different in its DNA. Starting with the first building block of organizing, the one-on-one conversation, your goal is to show your respect for your co-workers.

You're inviting them into the process of building a powerful, democratic union—one where their values, their experience, their ideas, and their contributions matter. You're inviting them to become a fellow organizer.

BUILD RELATIONSHIPS OF SOLIDARITY

When you talk to your co-workers as an organizer, your goal is not to become friends, though that may happen. And you're not trying to build relationships only with people who share your values or political views, though you may find some and consider them allies.

What you are doing is attempting to build relationships of solidarity. You and your co-workers might be different in lots of ways that could divide you, such as race, gender, age, or job title; it's easy to get caught up in who you like or don't like, who's a good worker or a slacker, who is a suck-up, who is ambitious or lazy, who is helpful or toxically competitive, on and on.

"We all work for the same employer, so we are bound to one another."

But despite all these judgments there is a single bottom-line fact that, once recognized, can bring workers together: "We all work for the same employer, so we are bound to one another. If we want to change anything here, our best hope is in working together."

Developing this understanding of our common interest is the key to overcoming divisions. The strength that workers have is our numbers and our unity. To build power, we'll need to build relationships with all sorts of people.

Be honest with people about why you're talking with them, and why you're so curious about their experiences and insights. For example: "*I don't think things are going well here. I want to solve problems. I want our union to be better.*" Does that sound like you have an ulterior motive? Quite the opposite. You're sharing your values and showing your honesty.

You can do all this—show respect, build a picture of who each co-worker is, and develop relationships of solidarity—all the time, with everyone, in your most casual and your most profound interactions.

BE CURIOUS

One of the most useful qualities an organizer can cultivate is *curiosity.* You actually want to know something about the person you're talking to.

For that you'll need to listen, rather than doing most of the talking yourself. Many organizers suggest that you listen 80 percent of the time and talk 20 percent. But curiosity goes deeper than that.

Really listen—and not just for an opening to make your pitch. Give yourself over to the kinds of questions you would ask if you were at a party, meeting someone you genuinely liked for the first time. Everything they're talking about is stuff you've been thinking about too. You keep asking questions because what they have to say is so compelling to you.

Really listen—and not just for an opening to make your pitch.

You don't have to fake it. People who are motivated to make their union more democratic tend to be curious about their co-workers, even those they don't much like. You are not going to like all of your co-workers, but you can still try to find something that connects you with them. Allow this warm interest in each and every co-worker to spring naturally from your commitment to building a stronger union.

ASK QUESTIONS PEOPLE CAN ANSWER

Start by asking people questions that they will know the answers to and can speak confidently about—like the questions Amy Calandrella asked in the elevator.

This doesn't necessarily mean asking people to list their problems at work. In fact, that may *not* be a question they can easily answer. Many people don't spend time thinking about problems because they don't think anything can be done to change things. They feel powerless.

So, in the beginning of the relationship, after you've gotten to know someone a bit—where they live, what's their family situation, what's important to them outside the job—it's good to let them tell you about their work. You could ask questions like:

- What do you do here?
- How long have you been here?
- How did you end up working here?
- What do you think about this place?
- What do you like about this job?
- Do you get to know the people you work most closely with?
- What do you think of the boss?
- What bothers you about working here?
- Are you thinking about leaving?

- Have you had better jobs or worse jobs in the past?
- Have you ever tried to do anything to improve things?
- What were the results of that?
- Who do you look up to in the workplace?
- Who do you trust?
- Who don't you trust?

None of this is small talk. All of it will help you get a sense of who this person is, in the context of this workplace. You are building up a picture of what it might take to invite this person into a collective process—that's your goal. Very often the minimum thing it would take is their feeling that there is someone in the union who has shown them some respect!

WHAT TO PAY ATTENTION TO AS YOU ARE ASKING QUESTIONS

The following pair of dialogues offers two contrasting versions of a conversation you might have with a co-worker early on—and as you begin to see that there's something they want to change about the workplace.

This scenario imagines that you're in a nonunion workplace. But you could take the same kind of approach in a unionized workplace.

In both examples, you're hoping to bring the worker into a process that leads toward collective action. But the first approach is an effort to lead your co-worker to a predetermined outcome. The second approach—the more effective one—is shaped by your respect for the worker's experience and what you're learning about their interests. The co-worker will feel the difference.

Example 1: Leading a co-worker toward a predetermined outcome

Q: What bothers you about working here?

A: It seems that new things are always being added to my list. Nothing taken off, just new duties added.

Q: Do you have a job description?

A: I don't know. I've never seen one.

Q: Could you ask for one?

A: I have no idea who I'd ask. My manager has only been here two months longer than me.

Q: Don't you think you need a job description?

A: I don't know. I've never had one, and I've worked six different jobs in the last 10 years.

Q: Probably it would be better if you had a job description, right? It would limit having new things added all the time.

A: I have no idea. If you say so.

Q: Did you know that if we had a union here, we could force management to write job descriptions and follow them?

A: I don't know about that. They seem to make up their own rules.

Q: Do you think some of your co-workers would be interested in a union? It would really give you power to change things.

A: [Shrug]

Example 2: Learning about a co-worker

Q: What bothers you about working here?

A: It seems that new things are always being added to my list. Nothing taken off, just new duties added.

Q: Can you give me an example?

A: Yesterday, I was stocking shelves and the manager told me I had to inventory a whole aisle of the store I'd never worked in before.

Q: What did you do?

A: I asked the manager for the stocking sheet for that aisle, but he gave me one that was six months old. It was really hard to complete it. Then he yelled at me for being slow.

Q: That's demeaning. Have you talked with any co-workers about this, about having new assignments piled on?

A: Oh yeah! We complain about it all the time.

Q: Have you ever talked about doing something to try and push back?

A: No way. Everyone's scared to say anything.

Q: Do you know three or four co-workers you could get together with—say, after work on a Friday—to just talk about it? What's everyone's experience, what are they scared of, whether there's something you could do about it?

A: Sure, we could talk. I don't know if it will do any good, but I can ask.

You are listening for a topic that really concerns them. In the first example, you leap in with your own solution. In the second example, you suggest getting a few people together to talk about a solution.

LISTEN FOR AN EXPRESSION OF UNION VALUES

Respect is about the character of the interaction; it's not about following a script. Good organizing begins with the belief that each co-worker has dignity, can think and plan, and can cooperate with others to fix problems.

Without this belief, we will default to expecting someone else to fix our problems—maybe the boss, maybe HR, maybe some charismatic politician. But that won't work, because in reality, these people are taking care of their own problems, not ours.

One way you might show your co-worker respect is by simply finding out how they're doing and especially *what* they are doing. It may seem that a co-worker is apathetic, clueless, or resigned to bad conditions. But in truth, nearly everyone will have tried something to protect themselves, improve things, or help others on the job.

You are looking for that special ingredient—it's going to be there in almost everyone you meet—that shows that they share a union value, such as compassion, cooperation, or independent thinking. When you see even a smidgeon of that, ask more about it!

Nearly everyone will have tried something to improve things or to help others on the job.

For example:

- I noticed you rolling your eyes when the supervisor was describing the new procedure. What was on your mind?
- You were really helpful when I ran into that problem. How did you figure that out?
- I saw you remind our new co-worker that she didn't have to take overtime work, even though the boss was pressuring her. How did that go?
- How do you manage to avoid all the cliques at work? It seems you're fair with everyone.

And keep it honest. Don't pander or flatter; just follow your own curiosity and respond to the leads you are offered in the conversation.

This kind of dialogue can be great for understanding your co-workers' values, motivations, and what they really care about. This is where you can find common ground and expand on it.

CHAPTER 2: ORGANIZE DEMOCRATICALLY

"Can We Even Do That?"

Two things surprised Basia Sokal when she arrived at her new job in a small-town post office in Nova Scotia: the warm welcome she received from her new co-workers, and how badly they were all being treated.

Sokal was already a seasoned union activist, a longtime letter carrier who had even been president of the labor council back in Winnipeg. She and her husband had just moved cross-country, and she got a job as a postal retail clerk while waiting for a letter carrier job to open up.

Sokal had heard that Nova Scotians could be insular—there's even a term for outsiders: They "come from away." So she was charmed when everyone clapped for her when she first arrived and made her feel welcome.

"But very quickly I found out, 'Wow, the boss has been taking advantage of these workers,'" Sokal said. She knew the letter carrier provisions of the contract well. Now every night she was reading the sections on retail workers. "I thought, 'Everything that's going on here is in complete violation of the collective agreement.'" She started bringing her copy of the contract into the post office, and people would ask her, "What's that?"

Another surprise: There was no functioning union local. "I was very disappointed to hear that, because I was excited to start participating," Sokal said. The regional union had taken temporary control of this local two years earlier, and there was no timeline for getting it back under member control.

After a rainstorm punched a hole in the post office roof, workers came in to discover that Canada Post had done a shoddy repair featuring a tarp, a garden hose, and a bungee cord. Water was dripping down the pillars. "People were telling me, 'It's a good thing we're wearing masks still, because of all this asbestos and mold,'" Sokal said. "I was like, 'It's time to call a complaint meeting about this.'"

"What is that?" her co-workers asked. "Can we even do that?" The contract gave union members the right to summon management to complaint meetings—but apparently here, it had never been done.

"I started taking concerns down on a sheet of paper," Sokal said, "which quickly turned into five to 10 sheets." When she asked for volunteers to speak in the complaint meeting, her co-workers nominated her. Sokal argued the speaker should be someone who knew this workplace well, not someone brand new. Eventually they reached a compromise: She would speak jointly with a co-worker who had been stuck in a perma-temp position for 10 years and was always overlooked.

The meeting went great. Afterward Sokal wrote up notes, and workers held a short meeting to review what management had committed to do, and by when. The best part: "The next week, people came in and said, 'I have an idea, I think we should do this,'" Sokal said. "It was amazing: they went home on the weekend and thought about it.

"That's when we really started to talk about, 'How are we going to organize this workplace? What is our game plan if A, B, and C happen, or if A, B, and C don't happen?'"

In the months she worked there, "I think we had three complaint meetings, and by the last one, I wasn't even in them," Sokal said. Her co-workers had picked up the ball and run with it. The organizing momentum grew from there into a movement to win back local control of the union.

"I always think of a relay race," Sokal said. "You're running to the next stop with this baton, and you pass it off to the next person. That's how I always feel unions should function. When you feel, 'I've got a good grasp on this,' it's time to bring somebody else along. Knowledge is meant to be shared."

"Knowledge is meant to be shared."

There is a democratic impulse to all organizing. We are wresting unilateral control away from the boss so that we have more say in our own lives.

But the best organizing is also *conducted in a democratic way*. Co-workers talk to each other, listen to each other, and make plans with each other. All the members, not just the officers, debate and decide what the group will do. This approach to organizing is not just morally righteous—it is also the way to build the most power.

ABOUT POWER

The Labor Notes book *Democracy Is Power,* by Martha Gruelle and Mike Parker, begins by listing six themes:

- **Union power requires democracy.** Unions need active members to be strong, and people won't stay involved for long if they don't have control of the union's program.
- **The workplace (not the union hall) is the starting point for union democracy,** because the purpose of democratic control in the union is to be more effective against the boss. If members choose and organize their own job actions, they'll bring that power into union meetings.
- **No set of rules can guarantee democracy.** When we talk about democracy we mean much more than, for instance, fair election procedures—although rules are important tools. Democracy means a culture of control by the members.
- **Racism and sexism are still barriers to union democracy.** We can't just remove explicit discrimination and be done; democratic unions consciously and actively strive to include everyone.
- **Working people are fit to run our own affairs.** We are intelligent, can act cooperatively, and

are fully capable of analyzing our situation and crafting the best strategy to improve it. Given real choices, we can overcome our prejudices and work for the betterment of all.

- **Members have the right to organize around a view of how to run the union.** This means more than the right to voice opinions. We have the right to work with others who agree to convince still more to come along. This is the essence of building a reform movement in a union.

TAKE DEMOCRACY SERIOUSLY

A rank-and-file approach to organizing takes democracy seriously. You're inviting your co-workers into a process where they *feel* respected… because they *are* respected. In the union, someone's going to listen to them—and that doesn't just mean you're going to nod your head. What they have to say can be a valuable contribution.

In some of our unions, members recognize that there's no way in. They have questions no one is going to answer, or they don't trust the answers they are given. They feel they're being moved like pieces on a chessboard, or assigned makework tasks to test their commitment or influence. When they try to join the group that makes the plans, they are rebuffed.

Unions with a democratic spirit do better than this. We want people to stay for the long haul, not just be pawns. That's how we build our collective power. So in a democratic union:

- Members can and should talk with their co-workers about anything related to their work.
- Members have access to information about the union—its finances, its policies, how decisions are made, how to get in touch with other members.

- Union conversations are not just complaining—they're productive conversations that lead somewhere.
- Members can contribute meaningfully and help develop plans of action. Think of Basia Sokal's complaint meeting: Workers compiled the list of complaints together, confronted management together, and met afterward to plan their next steps together.
- Organizing—that is, bringing people together to make plans and act collectively in the name of the union—is something that any member can do. It's not the exclusive role of people with official titles. The more people start organizing, the stronger the union becomes.

Organizing is something that any member can do.

GROUP DISCUSSION IS WHERE THE MAGIC HAPPENS

Democracy isn't only about how a union's formal structures operate. It's also about whether members can operate democratically on the shop floor as organizers.

Though one-on-one conversations are an essential building block of organizing, your goal should always be to springboard from one-on-ones to group dialogue. Try to move people in the direction of talking with each other in groups as often as possible.

Every issue will affect some people more than others—whether it's an issue at work, like an awful new schedule, or in the union, like trying to get a resolution passed. Maybe it's all the workers in the department, or all the union delegates.

The first task is to find the people who are affected and help them come together and talk. Can we agree on a concrete goal? What will it take to achieve it? What action is this group willing to take—and could it be enough to win our demand?

> Your goal should be to springboard from one-on-ones to group dialogue.

Since you're eager to get stuff going, don't be surprised if you're the one tossing out the most ideas at first. But you have to be prepared for your co-workers to reject your ideas. Get over your own ego. Be ready to say, "OK, the ideas I put out don't make sense. Let's talk about what *does* feel possible to you and our other co-workers." You'll repeat that pivot over and over again.

If you find that the initial group does *not* have the capacity to achieve its goal, ask: Who is the next circle of people we can invite into this process? And can we agree that we should be open to redefining our goal as we include more people?

For example, say three people in your worksite agree that the supervisor is a bully. The three of you talk it over: "*What can we do to deal with this bully?*" But that leads to another question: "*Will it be enough if the three of us take some action?*" Together you conclude, "*No, but it would be different if 10 out of the 12 people he supervises did something.*" Now you've identified your next circle of people to talk to.

The goal might change as a result. Maybe 10 people aren't ready to try to get the supervisor fired, but all 10 will push for a face-to-face meeting with him. Flexibility is the necessary attitude.

This approach doesn't necessarily mean you'll end up with a watered-down demand. Maybe with new input the group will come up with a whole different way of seeing and addressing the issue. Or maybe with greater numbers and a slower timeline, enough people will feel emboldened to take a stronger action.

Maybe the 10 people *will* ultimately try to get the supervisor fired—but in order to build enough unity for that, you might have to exhaust milder measures together first. Don't be scared of going slow; just be committed to going forward.

DEMOCRACY DOESN'T MEAN ENDLESS MEETINGS

Organizing democratically means there is group consultation going on all the time. But you don't have to (and usually shouldn't expect to) have 90 percent of members come to a union meeting.

We've all heard—or made—this complaint: "We just can't get enough people to come to the meeting." We picture a democratic decision as one where everybody gets in a room together, debates, and then votes.

The truth is, a big meeting often isn't realistic, for reasons we all understand. Everybody is working hard, their schedules are staggered, they live far apart, their lives are complicated and exhausting. Plus, people may have gone to union meetings before and found them boring or unproductive.

So your consultation with members will often take another form. It could be a small group of leaders going out and having conversations, then coming back together and consolidating information, then going out again, with the idea of having a big meeting a month later.

Approach the process with transparency—let everyone know who you're talking with, why you're talking with them, and that everyone you talked with already is going to hear about it before any decision is reached. Make no promises about the outcome, and don't carry your own inflexible agenda. Instead, listen to what you're hearing, and try to identify the points of unity among the largest cohort.

Unity has to be built. That's one reason not to rely too much on surveys that ask each individual about their own priorities (see page 240). An organizer's aim is to help people talk to one another and think critically about everyone's needs and opinions, not just their own.

The point of inviting people into a process is not just to make them feel invested, but also to incorporate their ideas. Goals, tactics, and strategy may change as a result of bringing more people in, and that's good in the long run.

INVITE PEOPLE TO THINK TOGETHER

Access to decision-making is the most powerful invitation we can extend. It's commonly understood that in organizing our goal should be to offer people things to do—we want them to feel needed, so we give them small achievable tasks. That's fine, but the one skill we should always be inviting people to develop is their skill as critical thinkers.

Whatever anybody is doing as part of a union effort or organizing campaign—even if it's just picking up doughnuts for the picket line—it's an opportunity for some questions and dialogue. And it's a chance to develop critical thinking together. That's how people go from feeling like "I'm only good for picking up doughnuts" to "I'm part of a network of people who are thinking about how we keep building our power."

You might say to that doughnut-bringer, "Can you stick around and talk for 15 minutes afterward? All the people who are taking care of food for the picket lines are getting together to talk about how things are going, what's ahead for next week, what you're hearing, or any problems that have come up." After all those visits to the picket lines, people are likely to have good insights not only about the food, but also about the strike itself.

RESIST SHORTCUTS

Don't be seduced by the promise of "efficiency" and begin to make the important decisions with just a small group of the most dedicated people. That undermines the democratic spirit of an organization.

A hospital workers union under new leadership started considering whether bargaining units in the same sector or industry could bargain together instead of separately, since the union has more power that way.

But there was suspicion and distrust between groups that were not familiar with each other. Members in some units thought, "We've got to look out for ourselves," or "If we have to share, we'll get less."

Some of the presidents of these bargaining units had been moving in the direction of joint bargaining for years. But instead of going ahead just because they thought it was a good idea, they started an education process. They talked with members in each bargaining unit about the idea, working it through: "What would this mean? What are your concerns?"

> Don't be seduced by the promise of "efficiency."

They also began bringing members together for social events. When there was a strike in the area, they brought members of different units out to the picket line and introduced them, then set up regular contract study sessions where members looked at one another's contracts to see what they had that others didn't.

It's not a question of authority. The executive board of your union may have the authority to make a decision. But if you want to build power, you should always be reaching out and consulting others.

HOW CAN UNION STAFF HELP BUILD A DEMOCRATIC UNION?

Organizing is a collective activity. So everyone who organizes—whether a rank and filer, elected officer, or union staffer—has to be careful not to get bossy. This is something union staffers should be especially conscientious about, because the members should run the show.

Whatever the problem you're setting out to confront—member apathy, division inside the union, a bad boss, a contract campaign—members need to be involved in developing the solution and planning what to do. Be careful not to prejudge the solution.

If you're a union staffer, begin by finding out who's already aware of a workplace problem, and get members talking to each other. Your job in the conversation is to turn what may seem to workers like a dead end or an endless cycle of wheel-spinning—"we've tried that, it hasn't worked, no one cares"—into a clear goal, with some dose of optimism, or at least a commitment to try something.

Get members talking and working with one another, not just with you. Encourage members to figure out who else is likely affected by the problem and how to bring them into the conversation. You can help them prepare and practice what to say to their co-workers.

The organizer's task is to prepare people to have their own conversations.

Maybe a small group agrees to do a face-to-face survey. When you come back together, now instead of having five people who are concerned, we've talked to 50, and wow, 87 percent said their problem was x. Maybe they write up the results, go back out to check in with people again, and then hold a meeting.

Again, you might role-play or talk through how to frame the issue. The organizer's task is to prepare people to have their own conversations with each other. That's where the democratic process happens.

It's not as if you (the organizer or staff person) are invisible. You may have experience, expertise, and ideas that will be very valuable. Members who are not experienced organizers might have an idea of what they want, but it's not something that can be achieved. So you certainly should ask questions, offer cautions, and suggest possible actions or strategies.

(If you as a union staffer are not permitted to support bottom-up decision-making, what do you do? See page 217.)

> Things may go in a different direction than you expected. They may take a lot longer and be a lot messier. But the result will be authentic and powerful. The question for you as a staff member is how detached you can be from controlling the outcome.

CHAPTER 3:
STAY GROUNDED IN REALITY

ONE
ONE

The Winding Road to Reform in an Auto Workers Local

Scott Houldieson has been fighting for a better union the whole 36 years he's been an electrician at the Chicago Ford assembly plant, and he's gotten slammed by reality more times than he can count.

In his United Auto Workers local, Houldieson has been elected alternate committee person, financial secretary, and vice president. But he has also lost elections to rivals who consolidated power by doling out favors and punishments. "Even if I wasn't elected," he said, "I always go to meetings, listen to reports, watch the executive officers. Serve as a check and balance."

He has learned to take setbacks in stride, assess what's possible in a changing landscape, and keep putting one foot in front of the other.

By 2019, the news was full of a horrifying corruption scandal inside the UAW. Top leaders of the international union had been colluding with the automakers to steal funds from workers for their personal benefit. For years, many had suspected this was happening—but suddenly it was out in the open, and union leaders were being charged.

Houldieson had kept in touch over the years with members who believed the union could be more militant and democratic. Now he and others finally saw an opening to push for direct elections of top officers—the same remedy that rank-and-file Teamsters had used years ago to successfully challenge corruption in their union. It was a long shot, but it was worth a try.

Houldieson helped found the reform caucus Unite All Workers for Democracy. At first the activists worked to pass local resolutions calling for a special convention to amend the union constitution. But their plans were disrupted by the pandemic: In-person union meetings were canceled, and the momentum to pass resolutions stalled.

The caucus then refocused its attention on the federal corruption investigation, and began urging the government to institute direct elections. The government settled instead on a referendum—members would vote on whether they wanted the right to vote.

"We were disappointed, but it turned out to be a gift," Houldieson said. "The referendum forced us to organize." If the government had simply imposed a direct election, he said, it "would not have forced us to reach out to members of our union to collect contact info and find like-minded people."

By the time the referendum passed, UAWD was better prepared to recruit candidates and campaign for office. The UAWD-backed slate led by Shawn Fain won, and immediately began building toward a strike at the Big 3.

Houldieson didn't wait for directions from the new leaders. He started organizing contract actions every week or two in his plant: "This was really a critical opportunity to show what power we had."

Because of Houldieson's activism, the local leadership put him on the strike committee. "When I asked how many other people were on the strike committee, they said nine. I said this wasn't enough." He mapped out the factory, identifying potential recruits from every shift and department, enough to cover the plant. The committee grew to 100 members, 30–40 of them very active.

The international's new leaders hadn't yet sent out directions on contract campaign trainings. So Houldieson's local found some materials and held a training anyway. "We caught hell for not following protocols from our regional leadership," Houldieson said. "But the trainings brought many members in. When other levels of the union weren't ready, we just went ahead and got started."

After the wildly successful Stand-Up Strike at the Big 3 in 2023, Houldieson is still working to strengthen his local, as co-chair of the organizing committee. "My idea is to expand our organizing capacity by increasing the number of members who are involved," he said. "We're trying to shift the paradigm so the members themselves can help take on this task, to build the union from the bottom up."

Organizing isn't just about thinking and talking, it's also about doing. And the minute we start doing, we are engaging with—and hopefully changing—the reality around us.

Our goal as worksite organizers is to shift power—to win more of it for the workers—so that our lives can be more decent, more dignified, and more under our own control. But we have to start with a clear-eyed view of how things really are, and plan accordingly.

As the song says, "You gotta know when to hold 'em and know when to fold 'em." For most of his career, Scott Houldieson wisely assessed that he could make the most headway by focusing his organizing energies on the local level. But when conditions shifted, he seized the chance to build an ambitious campaign to change the UAW International.

When the pandemic hit, Houldieson also recognized the need for tactical shifts. And when he joined the strike committee, he soberly assessed that preparing his big plant for a strike would require 100 reps, not nine. That enabled him and his team to set clear priorities: map the plant, find the reps, cover the whole workplace, then prep for the strike.

Checking reality—being curious, clear, and honest about what is happening—will enable you to find trustworthy allies, strengthen communication among co-workers, choose winnable battles, avoid dead ends, and keep up morale.

All it requires is that you keep your eyes open, notice things, ask questions, reflect and evaluate with others, and don't jump to conclusions. It should be part of what you are doing all the time, not just once and done. Here are a few areas to reality-check as you organize.

EVALUATE COMPLAINTS

Everyone complains about work. Complaining sometimes seems like the glue that holds a workplace together. It's tempting to slide into gripe mode, because agreeing about how bad things are helps you fit in and make friends.

But as organizers, we need to figure out if a complaint is about a real problem or not. Does the complaint help us understand the reality of the workplace, or distort it? What's behind the complaint: a desire to make things better, some kind of personal vendetta, or just empty talk with no real purpose?

We can't, and shouldn't, jump on every complaint—but we can learn how to discern the reality and utility of a complaint. Instead of cultivating the camaraderie of shared resentment, it's better for a worksite organizer to ask questions to uncover what's behind the complaint.

A union organizer newly assigned to a nursing home with a wall-to-wall bargaining unit—including housekeepers, dietary workers, drivers, social workers, nursing assistants, and nurses—was pummeled by a steady onslaught of complaints from members in every department, accompanied by assertive denials that anything could change.

The organizer didn't just take it all at face value. Instead, she sought out the complainers and asked questions: *When did this thing you're complaining about start? What led to it? Who is affected by it? Who do you think is responsible? Has anything been tried to fix it? What change would you like to see? Do others share your opinion? Does anyone disagree with you about this?* She looked for themes.

What she saw was a lot of finger-pointing at workers in different job titles. The housekeepers grumbled that the food service workers left big messes, never put things away, and spilled so much that the floor was a hazard. Nursing assistants seethed with resentment that nurses left them with the dirty work and were never available to advise how to work with the residents. On and on.

The next step was to feed back her observation to the workers—she suggested that they were aiming at each other when they could be coming together to aim at the boss. Maybe the kitchen staff needed better staffing, additional storage space to put things away, longer shifts (with a pay differential), or overlapping shifts to handle the workload. Maybe the nursing assistants and nurses needed time built into their workdays to consult about their patients, more in-service education, greater clarity about how to divide tasks, and more people to do the work.

In this case, the complaints had to be unpacked to find where the blame could productively be placed.

Unpack complaints to find where the blame can productively be placed.

PAY LESS ATTENTION TO THE BOSS

How obsessed are your co-workers with the boss?

Do all gripe sessions start and end with what the boss is or isn't doing? The complaint could be about what she said, in what tone of voice, and with what implied insult or threat. Or it could be about how he never listens, or she listens but never follows up, or he's never around, or she's surrounded by suck-ups.

These complaints may be true. But if they become excuses for not doing something to improve the workplace, then you are giving the boss's actions too much weight and power.

Any group of workers that can't think beyond the boss's personality is likely to stay disorganized, disempowered, and disappointed. The boss is just doing their job, which is to hoard power and control workers. We shouldn't help them by allowing them to dominate our thoughts and actions.

Encourage your colleagues to give more attention to each other—to look out, not up.

Encourage your colleagues to give more attention to each other—to look out, not up. It's the relationships we build with each other that change the balance of power.

A group of workers at a commercial tree nursery could not get their employer to set a schedule for summer work. Everyone was entitled to a week's vacation, and they had put in their requests by the deadline, but he wasn't making a schedule. Plans for travel, graduations, weddings, and family reunions were all on indefinite hold—and their frustration fused into obsession about the boss and his failings. Rather than trying to fix the problem, all anyone could talk about was how angry they were at him.

Eventually one of the workers who had some organizing instincts went to each co-worker and wrote down which week they wanted off. Then she got everyone together on a lunch break, while the boss was out of town, and they hammered out a schedule that everyone could live with. Then they presented it to him as the schedule they intended to follow.

No response. Had they gone too far? Was he so angry that he was going to fire them all? But in a week, the summer schedule was posted—exactly as they had designed it.

Once a solid network of co-workers has come together to take action to solve a problem, you can start thinking about the boss in a new light. He is no longer the one with all the power, who must be obeyed and resented, but a target against whom you can bring pressure—or possibly even someone you can overrule with a plan of your own.

SEEK OUT UNLIKELY ALLIES

You may feel like you're alone in your desire to build a fighting, democratic union. You may encounter co-workers who are anti-union, union officers who act like bullies, and cynical colleagues who scorn your efforts to improve anything. Some people in your workplace may be reactionary or racist. That's common: After decades of anti-union propaganda spewing from politicians and corporate elites, the general climate can be pretty bleak.

Focus on co-workers who show some values and a spark of optimism.

But if you do a reality-check, you might realize that focusing on the toxic naysayers is a dead end. Instead, focus on co-workers who show some values and a spark of optimism. Who shows up with integrity, compassion, or courage? Is there someone you turn to for the "straight story" when you're in doubt? Who is well-informed without being a know-it-all? Who refrains from gossip? What friendship circles provide resiliency? Was there a time when a group of co-workers took a stand together? Can you connect with them?

You're not necessarily looking for co-workers who share your political views, but rather, those who might share goals for a better contract, a less oppressive workplace, or a more powerful union.

FIND AN ACCESSIBLE WAY IN, OR BUILD YOUR OWN WAY

If meetings in your union are deadening—perhaps you're lectured to and given no time for discussion—you might find that trying to change those meetings is beating your head against the wall.

Often, people who are beginning an effort to transform their union identify a few like-minded people and bring them to a union meeting, only to find that the meeting is so boring or offputting that the new recruits never want to attend a union meeting again.

If you go to a space that is dead and you don't have the power to make it undead, don't focus your organizing on inviting others there. Instead, consider recruiting them to a union committee that offers a chance for real participation and action.

Scott Houldieson considered it useful to observe boring union meetings so he could offer "checks and balances." But he put more energy into welcoming other members into more dynamic settings like a strike committee, an organizing committee, or contract campaign trainings.

If union stewards are hand-picked by a president who doesn't want any controversy in "his" union (and so won't fight for the members), then perhaps it's time to assemble a network of worksite activists who can support members in day-to-day skirmishes with supervisors—even without the title of steward.

MATCH YOUR GOALS TO YOUR POWER

Our aspirations are big, but our power may be small. Forcing our national union to strike against two-tier pay might not be in the cards this year. But how about starting with something smaller that matters to people, like getting management to fix the broken ventilation system that drives shop floor temperatures into the nineties all summer?

Don't spend too much time setting grandiose goals that you can't reach now, or writing the perfect program that includes everyone's maximum demand. Instead, make plans that can succeed, and then build on that success to set bigger goals. Keeping a clear eye on the reality of your existing power is essential to growing it.

> When you win a small fight, it attracts more people to join your organizing.

You may feel that you have to choose a really big thing. You might dismiss small goals as inadequate and therefore unimportant. Often lofty goals are based on a correct analysis of the situation: Two-tier pay is a profound injustice, the root of many other problems, and a rallying issue among our co-workers.

But if you jump into action aiming for a goal that's way beyond your power to achieve, then you'll either experience a constant sense of defeat and demoralization or you'll feel boxed into overselling modest results as victories. Either way, it can lead to burnout.

Are you limited to small goals forever? No. When you win a small fight, it attracts more people to join your organizing and builds your collective power so you can set your sights a bit higher the next time. This process is usually slow, with setbacks. But over time, accumulating small wins is a more effective path to building power than magical thinking.

NO ONE CAN DO EVERYTHING

Organizers often find themselves exhausted: *I'm working too hard, there are too many demands on my time, and I'm overwhelmed by all that I'm expected to do.* Taking on too many things at once is not a helpful or effective strategy.

It's hard to choose priorities—but it's essential. Assess how much gas is in the tank and drive to the next stop. If you keep zipping around to every stop on the map, you'll soon be on "empty."

It's hard to choose priorities—but it's essential.

Organizers tend to be motivated by our values. All around us are problems screaming to be solved: poverty wages, layoffs, racism, climate change. Until you check the impulse to fix everything at once, you will be running around barely touching on each problem, giving none of them the benefit of your full attention.

Even worse, you will create an environment of frantic activity and desperation, which will have bad effects on you and your co-organizers. Some will think that's just what organizing looks like. They may pick up your problematic habits—or even back away from organizing altogether, thinking "I can't live like that."

And if you actually achieve a goal but it feels overshadowed by the many other problems that still loom, this too teaches an unappealing lesson—that organizers are constantly discouraged and unsatisfied.

Many of us have one eye on a wider horizon. The reason we're fighting the small battles is because we are ultimately aiming at a labor movement that can transform society. That's great, and it may sustain you to find community with others who share your politics, talk about grander goals and possibilities, and put your experiences in the perspective of a long-term struggle.

But an expansive vision should be your inspiration and moral compass, not a bludgeon you wield against yourself because your current efforts are on a smaller scale. Taking it one step at a time is the only way to get there.

DOES THE PLAN NEED ADJUSTING?

In our work as organizers, we are always setting goals, making plans, and constructing timelines. This orderliness is useful, and it can be reassuring to have ways to measure our progress. But reality is not orderly; it is extremely messy, with constant and unpredictable change.

In order to stay grounded in reality, a good guide is to stick to our intentions—the long-term goal to build worker power in the workplace—but be flexible and adaptive as conditions change. Pay attention to those changing conditions, and invite creative responses.

Scott Houldieson, in the story at the beginning of this chapter, demonstrates the flexibility a long-haul organizer must have. When he and other reform organizers saw a window of opportunity, they tried various strategies to achieve direct elections—at first organizing for a union convention, then pursuing a legal strategy aimed at the federal government, and ultimately winning enough votes in a member referendum. In his local, he hasn't fixated on his own ambitions to retake union office but instead has taken opportunities to build collective strength, pouring his efforts into a strike committee and then an organizing committee.

Imagine that your local is in contract negotiations and you've been recruited to chair a Contract Action Team. The members of the CAT agree on a goal: getting union members strike-ready within six months.

You've spent a few meetings mapping out a timeline in which you will identify a CAT captain in every department, assess what members think about the possibility of a strike, plan actions to highlight specific contract demands, and put out strike Q&As to anticipate fears members have, all leading to a strike authorization vote when it is needed.

But then the bargaining team throws on the brakes, fearing that strike talk will sour the negotiations. Your CAT is ordered to cease and desist.

This doesn't mean giving up or dissolving in frustration. It means reassessing the current reality: Can the CAT meet with the bargaining team to change their minds? Is it possible to build a modified timeline, focusing on outreach and engagement at the worksite, but hold off on discussing a strike for a while? Could the CAT just concentrate on one-on-one conversations and small-group meetings to build commitments around certain demands that can likely only be won with a strike? In short, can the CAT keep its original goal in mind while adjusting the plan?

This flexible approach is helpful for all goals you might set. For example, a caucus has the goal of getting a good contract. They run a candidate for the bargaining team, but she loses. The overall goal is still to get a good contract, so the group adjusts its plan and figures out how this member and others can contribute to the fight as rank-and-file organizers in their departments. No effort is wasted, as long as you can keep framing new ways to reach your goal.

Our job is to face reality and see how that current reality can inform us in setting our next steps.

CONSTANTLY REASSESS THE SHIFTING BALANCE OF POWER

We tend to measure success in union work based on the material outcome of a specific struggle: Did we win a raise that's higher than inflation? Did we prevent the erosion of our health insurance plan? Did we get protection against mandatory overtime?

Tallying up what you won isn't always the best way to measure success.

But tallying up what you won isn't always the best way to measure success. Some of your gains may slip away to inflation, or to the employer's cheating, or members may not be able to take full advantage of the wins. (Picture the worker who won't take the contractual 10-minute rest break because it would look like they were slacking.)

An equally important measure of success is who brought about that material improvement. If it was gained in a backroom deal with the boss or effected by the union lawyer or an officer with no other member involved, members may get the idea that power lies with these people, not with workers themselves.

Ask the question: *Has the balance of power in the workplace shifted away from the boss and toward the workers?* This can be measured in how workers feel about themselves, about each other, about the workplace, and about the job.

If a group mounts some kind of collective resistance, even on a small scale—for example, resisting a bad policy, stressful working conditions, or a monster of a supervisor—ask how people are feeling afterward. If there's a sense of increased confidence, more respect among co-workers, less fear of the boss, then the balance of power has shifted. This is a foundation to build on.

CHAPTER 4: STAY STEADY

ULP
STRIKE
TEAMSTERS

A Teamster Finds Shoulders to Lean On

When he was a teenager in East New York, Antonio Rosario saw how easy it would be for his life to spin out of control.

His mother was struggling to keep them afloat by caring for children and the elderly. Rosario knew that in his neighborhood, a young guy like him could make faster money stealing cars or dealing drugs. But after witnessing a grisly incident, he was convinced that such a route could get him killed. "If I died or went to jail, who would be there for my mom?" he said.

At 20, while attending community college, Rosario heard about a job opportunity from a classmate who was nodding off in class after an exhausting shift sorting packages at UPS. He went for it.

The work was hard. As a part-time pre-loader, "you're touching 900 boxes a night, in the heat of August," he said. "I was busting my hump." But it was an honest living: "I wouldn't have to worry about looking over my shoulder."

A co-worker started telling Rosario about the union, Teamsters Local 804. "It didn't mean anything to me at first," Rosario said, and a union meeting left him unimpressed: "They seemed like a bunch of old white guys."

But he caught the bug at a rally. It was 1997, and the union was escalating to a national strike. "The energy was infectious," he recalled. "I'd never experienced anything like this before." The crowd roared as hometown hero Teamsters President Ron Carey declared, "We're hitting the streets!"

Rosario was working two UPS part-time jobs by then, trying to help his mom pay the mortgage and "not really making it." He asked his fellow Teamsters: Was a guy like him expected to strike? In response, he got an earful: "You think you're the only one who's struggling?" his co-workers said. "We've got families too."

"The 15 days of that strike was the most profound, impactful experience of my life."

"At that moment, I discovered it's all of us," Rosario said. In fact, guys like him gave that strike its theme: "Part-Time America Won't Work."

Rosario loved the picket line. "Give the kid the bullhorn," his local president said, and they did. "I was going in Spanish and English," Rosario said. "I was on fire. The 15 days of that strike was the most profound, impactful experience of my life."

Afterward, Rosario got more involved in the union. But when Teamsters President Carey, who had led the strike and the union's resurgence, was removed from office over campaign finance issues, Rosario lost heart. "Maybe we can't take on the world," he thought. "Maybe we just protect the contract, hunker down."

He says he kept that attitude all through his thirties. "I was pretty quiet, just staying back. It took me a long time to see that wasn't the right plan."

Rosario was finally drawn back into the fight when his local fell into the hands of officers whose actions he found intolerable. "They were giving their own guys benefits that violated the contract," he said. "I knew that was wrong. I had to start using my voice. I was tired of backpedaling, tired of playing defense.

"I didn't realize how many people agreed with me until I started speaking," Rosario said. "Then I saw that the point wasn't only to talk at members, but to listen to them." He started meeting with a few workers over lunch. After he changed the venue to playing basketball in the park, the group grew to 15 to 20. "I guess it was my first organizing experience."

Soon Rosario was helping organize an effort to replace the executive board. "We put together a really diverse slate—different jobs, several Black members, a Puerto Rican member. I started going from building to building for the slate, and Teamsters for a Democratic Union was organizing phone-banking. Then I went to a TDU conference and I thought, 'These are my people. I just didn't know it.' At TDU I found people who could help me learn how to organize, and I saw there was something we could really do."

The local reformers won, and Rosario went on to help elect new international leadership and build another UPS contract battle. In 2024, 30 years after becoming a Teamster, Rosario, now a TDU co-chair, found himself working for the union as an organizer, helping young Amazon workers plan a strike of their own.

"Sometimes you need to let other people help you think about things in a different way."

What keeps him going? "I have good people around me," Rosario said. He recalls how, during that Amazon strike, he experienced "a real low on the roller-coaster." An influential worker he had grown close to decided to cross the picket line—and Rosario couldn't change the man's mind. "I felt like he stabbed me and twisted the knife," Rosario said. Afterward he stood staring into space, tears welling in his eyes.

Then a younger organizer came over and said, "For every one they take from us, we'll win 10 more."

"That's all I needed," Rosario said. The strike "wasn't perfect—but the feel of the camaraderie is the really important lesson."

During the same strike, Rosario got arrested for a few hours. Once released, he headed straight back to picketing. "I was completely exhausted, couldn't keep my head up," he said. But he kept fighting it, making coffee, insisting he was OK even as his whole team urged him to go home.

"Look over there at the picket line," the lead organizer said. "The workers are totally running it. They own it. They have it. You helped them learn how to organize. Now you need to trust them and go take care of yourself."

She was right. "When you feel like you're hitting bottom, you have to have a support team," Rosario said. "They will be there for you. Sometimes you need to let other people help you think about things in a different way. I find that talking with both an older mentor and a younger organizer is really helpful.

"And get some sleep. Don't let more coffee carry you through. I had to learn it the hard way."

Some people get involved in organizing because they feel desperate, caged in, or frustrated at work. Some are furious at how mismanaged the workplace is, or how badly their co-workers are treated. These feelings may get us started—but they can't carry us through the long haul it takes to change the balance of power.

Organizing isn't about satisfying our emotional needs. It's about challenging the inequalities that make life hard for so many of us, and trying to create a decent and dignified world instead.

It's hard to keep going in the long run—and often both confusing and emotionally demanding. If you're signing up for the long haul, you can help yourself by learning how to stay steady.

GET OFF THE ROLLER COASTER

If you've tried organizing, chances are you've experienced surges of excitement and confidence... and bouts of exhaustion, confusion, disappointment, and hopelessness. Antonio Rosario's story features both the highs and the lows. Let's examine some of the problems of being on the emotional roller coaster, and how to get off that dizzying ride.

If you organize by whipping up people's emotions, generating enthusiasm, and perpetually creating momentum, you're taking on a heavy burden. How will you sustain that effort when you and your co-workers are facing awful working conditions, rigid bosses, and bleak prospects?

Sometimes organizers feel stumped by this, and end up playing cheerleader to generate engagement—declaring every fight the fight of the century, and every small victory historic. That may work once or twice, but when things don't greatly improve as a result of this supposedly historic win, members may get discouraged and fade away.

If you organize by perpetually creating momentum, you're taking on a heavy burden.

Even with a well-planned campaign that does generate momentum and produces a win, how can you avoid a sense that this now must be endlessly repeated to maintain members' confidence? You may be left feeling: *What can we do to top that?*

A tricky letdown can follow when feelings have been running high, a confrontation has been built, and the aftermath hasn't been planned for. People may be very disappointed when life returns to normal. This emotional roller coaster can exhaust us without necessarily strengthening the union or developing the members' confidence in themselves.

Are these cycles inevitable? Definitely not. Other approaches are possible.

Don't rely on emotions to organize. When you're talking with your co-workers, don't set out to inflame their anger. If you're inviting them to examine what they hate about their job, do it so that you can better understand their conditions and needs. Refrain from stirring up resentments and rage.

Instead, share your own insights and ideas, focusing on next steps and actions. For example, you might say about an abusive manager: "*She sounds awful, but let's not waste time demonizing her. What impact does her treatment have, and how can we resist it?*"

DON'T LET THE BOSS DESTABILIZE YOU

Focus on planning and carrying out actions, rather than on how the boss reacts. The boss knows you're trying to provoke her, so if she's smart she will try to not react. As long as she appears unmoved, workers will feel increasing anger, frustration, disappointment, and powerlessness. That's a dangerous dead end.

Managers everywhere are being taught not to respond meaningfully to anything. This management strategy may take the form of: "*I'm so glad you brought that up. We've got a committee/task force. Come join it...*" Then you waste your time on that for months and nothing actually changes.

Another version goes like this: You make a demand, perhaps just asking a simple question, and immediately *you* become identified as the problem, and are targeted by the boss.

At the peak of an intense contract campaign, UPS drivers in Boston decided to confront a particularly abusive manager, Brian, who had been handing out discipline unfairly. They did it by all turning their backs on him in their morning meeting. "When everyone dispersed from the morning meeting, the smiles on the drivers' faces were priceless," reported shop steward John Capodanno. "Even though it had only lasted two minutes, it felt so satisfying and victorious."

But management's immediate reaction was to

double down—putting out the word that Brian would lead even more meetings. A reaction like this is meant to demoralize workers, flipping their newfound confidence into cynicism. In this case, it turned out to be a bluff. In the following weeks, Brian quietly disappeared from meetings—and more important, the number of disciplines plummeted.

More and more, the management strategy is just to stonewall. Instead of sitting tight and waiting for a response, you might be tempted to "bargain against yourself" by lowering your demand in hopes of finding something the boss will agree with. But once the boss knows you'll make concessions, why should they agree to anything? Hold firm. Let your fellow unionists know that it's the boss who is going rogue by failing to respond—and prepare for that.

You can help your co-workers face the boss's tricks in a few ways:

- Help co-workers anticipate the various reactions you may get from management (including no reaction), and plan what the union will do in each scenario.
- Keep your attention on your own plans, and evaluate whether they were carried out as the group hoped.
- Discuss whether members changed during the course of a campaign: Did they get more focused, less fearful, less distracted by hearsay and gossip? Are they more determined? What contributed to those changes? How can they be sustained?

- Consider whether the union was strengthened during the campaign. For instance, did new people get involved? Did people learn a new tactic? Did people who had been at odds find that they could trust each other? If so, how can such campaigns or practices become a regular feature of the union's work?
- Connect the current campaign to the idea that you are organizing over the long haul. Remind your co-workers that this is a continuing effort that reaches back in time and also ahead. It's an effort served best by steady commitment, not bursts of unsustainable energy.

BE A MAGNETIC EXAMPLE OF STEADINESS

Everyone who acts as an organizer is being watched and assessed by their co-workers. Organizing is not the normal status quo in most workplaces. So co-workers will wonder why you're doing this, whether you're trustworthy, what you're asking them to do, and whether it's sensible or safe.

The best way to build solid relationships is by *being* solid: calm, thoughtful, reliable, undaunted by setbacks, and not subject to drama. This also serves as a model for your co-workers.

If you are martyring yourself to organizing, or in a constant state of up and down, few others will want to take on the work you're doing. But showing that you can organize and maintain a balanced emotional presence is enticing. Take time to discover the amazing people who are your co-workers, and enjoy each other's company.

If you don't always *feel* calm and confident, that's normal. Try observing someone in your life who is steady—a co-worker, friend, family member, teacher, neighbor—anyone you have been able to watch over time. How do they respond in a crisis? Have they cultivated certain skills or a kind of discipline that strengthens them? What keeps them in balance?

Ask if you can talk more with them. Would they be willing to help "coach" you into a steadier state? This is something that can be learned, if you decide it's important.

SWEAR OFF DISAPPOINTMENT

Are you disappointed? Does it help?

Reality isn't what we hope for, it's just what is. Good organizers keep a productive attitude toward the actual conditions they face. Don't wallow in your anger, frustration, or disappointment about what isn't going the way you want. There's always something you can do, something to work with.

For example, if turnout at a meeting is low, people might say, "Where is everybody?" You might blame the people who didn't come, or blame yourself for not drumming up a stronger turnout. Either way, the blame game leads to disappointment, recrimination, and judging your co-workers. *We did all this work, but we didn't get the results we hoped for.*

Another attitude is possible: You walk into the room, and there are only a few people there. Don't ignore this fact, assign blame, or make excuses. Instead, you can make the best use of what the moment has brought you. Do a quick reassessment of the situation. If you have a smaller group, there are still things you can do.

You might say to those who have shown up: "Wow, thank you for showing up. We thought we might have more, but let's figure out what we can do given who's in the room." Maybe you had hoped to use the meeting to launch a petition drive for a cost-of-living increase. But given the smaller group, you say, "It looks like we're not quite ready to do that. Let's talk about some other steps we could take now to lay the groundwork for that effort."

With this approach, you're showing respect for everybody who's there, instead of making people feel like they wasted their time on a meeting that flopped. If people leave with a feeling that they've used their time productively, they're more likely to encourage co-workers to come the next time.

If you're disappointed in your co-workers for not attending, remember to reality-check. Maybe at first you assume that they're cynical or apathetic. But is it possible they're actually discouraged or afraid? If so, what could be done about this? It felt like a personal betrayal to Antonio Rosario when a particular Amazon worker crossed the picket line, but in reality the man was probably responding to heavy pressure from the boss and his own fears. Rosario found comfort in the solidarity he had built with other workers and organizers. The slow, steady work of building relationships with co-workers can be intimidating at first, but over time it becomes a source of satisfaction.

Another common source of disappointment is when other players on the field don't do as we hope. The media doesn't cover our struggle, or gets it all wrong. Other unions or community groups don't support our campaign. Politicians break their promises. Even some members of our own union disagree or undermine the goals we're fighting for.

Good organizers keep a productive attitude toward the actual conditions they face.

If unchecked, these disappointments can lead you to write off potential allies prematurely. We don't get to control how anyone else will react to us. We can only control how we react and what we do next.

Often novice organizers seize on the hope that politicians or the media will swoop in and save the day. Instead, focus first on your base—your own co-workers—because they are the ones who can build power with you over the long haul. The more you do that, the more likely you'll be able to attract media attention and win some political influence.

CONSTANTLY RETURN TO DEMOCRATIC VALUES

Organizing can put you through the wringer. Sometimes you'll feel frustrated at slow progress, disappointed by setbacks, or even angry with your co-workers. But your commitment to democratic values can sustain you through this hard work.

When you're feeling disappointed—in yourself, your co-workers, your boss's behavior, or how an organizing effort turned out—step back and consult your own values. What are they? Perhaps what draws you to organizing is a commitment to solidarity, fairness, equality, justice, compassion, or democracy. Why do you hold these values? Do they still seem as important as ever?

So long as your values are still intact, you have something solid to lean on. Antonio Rosario was heartbroken when Ron Carey lost the Teamsters presidency, but he never forgot the feeling of power when rank-and-file members had come together. When he experienced living under a different kind of local officer, who was rewarding his cronies and ignoring the regular members, he remembered that it didn't have to be this way. He was a little ashamed that he had kept his head down for so long, but he started over from scratch and found others who wanted to rebuild the kind of union they could be proud of.

It's OK if you find that your own skill level is not yet where you'd like it to be, or that people around you are not quite as responsible, accountable, or courageous as you are. All those are things that can be changed over time. Jump back in and stay in the fight.

If you consult your values and find a misstep, that's not the end of the world either—you just need to get back on track. A postal worker who was recently elected as clerk craft director in her local told me how, once she took on this role, she had started to develop the attitude that "they're my stewards, and I have to develop a program for them." One of the most active stewards pushed back: "No, everyone should have a say."

The new officer realized the steward was right—she valued democracy, and in her impatience she was losing track of that value. She wanted things to move faster, since there was so much to do, and she felt she had to push the stewards to do more. But the reminder to slow down for the sake of democratic input helped her adjust course.

It can be helpful to think about the people you encounter in your daily life, or have known over time. Ask yourself who stands out as someone you respect. What are their values? How have they shown compassion, courage, and confidence? Consider what has kept them going through the ups and downs of daily struggle. Ask them to have a conversation with you about how their beliefs sustain them. (Or, if they aren't available to you, imagine a conversation.)

These values are what give meaning to our lives and connect us to something bigger than ourselves. Use them as a lifeline when you feel like you're drowning.

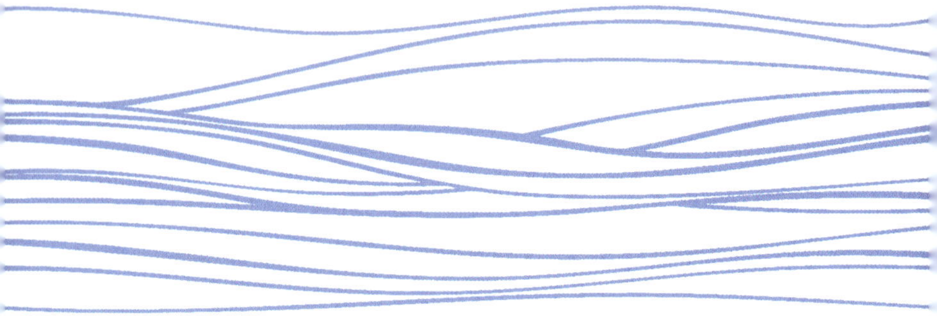

PART II: INGREDIENTS OF SUCCESSFUL ORGANIZING

The path of democratic labor organizing isn't smooth or linear, but it's as worthwhile as anything you're likely to try in life.

The following chapters describe four steps that can get you started and keep you going, even in the face of organizing dilemmas. Are they sequential steps? Not necessarily. Think of them instead as a checklist that you always keep in mind—and return to whenever your thinking gets a bit muddled about what to do next. The steps are:

- Help your co-workers understand power in the workplace.
- Overcome division and come together around common concerns.
- Overcome fear and take collective action.
- Reflect on the changing balance of power and keep going.

CHAPTER 5:
HELP YOUR CO-WORKERS UNDERSTAND POWER IN THE WORKPLACE

SOLIDARITY
ACTRA
TORONTO
LABOR NOTES

Actors Learn How to Steer the Ship

Kate Ziegler, a commercial actor in Toronto, never knew much about her union until the arrival of an alarming email.

It said that she and her fellow actors had been locked out by their employer, a business consortium called the Institute of Canadian Agencies. After one year of negotiations, the ICA was walking away from the bargaining table.

Ziegler had an upcoming job, recording a voiceover for national lottery commercials. "If I couldn't do the next recording date, it would wipe out a quarter of my income for the year," she said. "I had no idea things weren't going well. I had no idea how the contract worked."

She wasn't the only one. When union officials reluctantly called a town hall, horrified members demanded to know what had gone wrong in bargaining. They learned that the employers wanted the right to switch freely between union and nonunion work, and to cut some members' wages by 60 percent.

"When we heard that, more questions poured in," Ziegler said. "Why didn't we hear about this sooner—way sooner? I immediately began to fantasize about what could have happened if leadership had come to us the previous year saying, 'We have a big problem, we have to get prepared, we may have to strike.'"

As she learned more about how the employers were structured, she started analyzing what leverage the actors had. "I spent all day thinking about who we could go after to wrestle back some clients," she said. "Our paychecks are signed by the agencies, but the brands are the ones for whom the ads are being made. So why weren't we targeting the brands?"

But the union officials decided on a different strategy: doing informational picketing in front of ad agencies. Ziegler went to one of the pickets. "We noted quickly that no one was in the office," she said. "It was also a fairly quiet street, not visible. We felt like this couldn't possibly accomplish anything.

"I finally asked a union staffer, 'Whose idea was this? Why did no one ask the members? The members would know what might work.'

"A few of us organized a meeting with the union—about 100 members came—and we began to pepper the leadership with ideas. For example, the government does a lot of advertising, and they work with a lot of the agencies that locked us out. Let's shame them, expose the fact that they are supporting this lockout. Another possibility was McDonald's.

"I called local unions, labor councils, anyone I could find on the internet. Wouldn't their members want to know that the advertising agency their union uses was locking out other union members? I made a list of which unions used which agencies, and started to chart out a way to expose the way the money flows."

Fundamentally she felt her union was ignoring a critical power source: its own members' smarts and creativity.

Ziegler started to recognize other members on union Zoom calls who were asking similar questions. They formed a subcommittee and met with union officials. "But our ideas never went anywhere," she said. "Everything we wanted the union to do, they wouldn't or couldn't. So we decided to start meeting on our own, find our own resources, and build our own campaign."

She found the Labor Notes website and devoured materials on how to talk with your co-workers. She learned to "ask people how they are feeling, and identify what's the shared feeling."

"If my co-workers said they couldn't get involved—it's too messy, there's no hope it will change, I don't trust the union—I'd say, 'I can agree,' and then I'd ask, 'Why didn't we know what the union officers were planning? What in the world were they thinking? Did they want us to know? Did they *not* want us to know?'

"That would be very affirming to my co-workers, and it was the exact thing I wanted to talk with them about. Then the fear, frustration, and confusion started to recede. I would tell them, 'The union constitution says we're allowed to meet, we're allowed to ask questions and form our plans.' That's when people really got with the program."

The actors were learning about how their union worked, and also how it could work better. They were discovering that together they weren't so powerless, either to bring a real fight to their employers or to transform their union—and that these two projects went hand in hand.

Ziegler and the others formed a caucus, ran for office, and won a majority on the local union executive board. The lockout is still on. "But now members are showing up for rallies, events, town halls," Ziegler said. "They are feeling good that it's possible to start steering the ship."

An organizer's first job is to help their co-workers understand how power operates in the workplace and see themselves as part of a group that can change things.

In our economy, the nonunion employer has complete power over just about all working conditions. They create the job, hire, assign work, schedule work, promote, transfer, set wages, evaluate, hand out discipline, and fire.

Employees have zero say in any of those decisions—unless they have a union. And even if there is a union, workers may still feel like they and their co-workers have little or no say—unless there's a culture of organizing in the workplace.

This unbalanced power is so ingrained in our lives that few people question it. It's just assumed. Nonetheless, at some level, most workers resent it.

At one time or another, most of us feel that we're not paid well enough, listened to enough, or respected enough; that we don't have decent or dignified conditions at work—and that there isn't anything we can do about it, except complain or possibly quit.

If workers go on believing that the current balance of power is how it will always be, then organizing cannot succeed. You have to help your co-workers see that things can be different, even in very small ways.

Very few people will suddenly leap from feeling powerless to thinking, "I can take on the boss." Humans change little by little. And we most often change because someone around us has taken an interest in us and said, "Hey, have you considered this? What do you think about it?"

IT'S NOT PERSONAL

Most of us experience workplace problems as personal—they affect how we feel, and we tend to blame them on ourselves, our boss, or our co-workers. But to see how to remedy a workplace problem, we need to depersonalize the situation.

The problem isn't that your boss is a bad guy, personally (though maybe he is). It's not personal about you, either—your low pay or poor treatment is not because you're not smart enough or hard-working enough, or you haven't sucked up enough or made yourself sufficiently indispensable. Changing yourself to be what the boss needs is not the way to make things better.

> The problems you experience as personal are actually inevitable within our economic system.

The problems you experience as personal are actually inevitable within our economic system. Capitalism is based on competition; employers must compete with each other to drive down their own costs. Public and nonprofit employers operate on the same logic—they're often competing with for-profits, and run by people who went to the same business schools. So almost every employer pushes workers hard, tries to weed out the workers who push back, and uses all kinds of methods to control us. This power structure has been manufactured for a reason.

Depersonalizing allows you and your co-workers to see, "*Oh, it's not just me.*" The same problems are affecting most other workers. This recognition can make us feel less like victims, and more confident. Either we're all losers, or there's something being done to make us *feel* like we're all losers. Why and how are they doing it? Critical thinking can start to replace the habit of feeling victimized.

Does this change matter? You bet. In the long run, we can help co-workers develop the kind of critical thinking that's necessary to challenge capitalism's deep injustices. In the meantime, thinking critically helps us analyze our immediate situation and what to do about it so that we can act against the employer's tactics. *Why do bosses have to use guilt and manipulation to make me do my job? How does competition divide us and weaken us?* By talking these questions through, we become intellectually sharper and better able to challenge misuse of power.

IT'S UNDEMOCRATIC BY DESIGN

Most working people don't feel at all powerful. In fact, we are made to feel as powerless as possible. You may be called an "associate" or "partner" or "team member" by management, but just make a simple request for better treatment and see how far that label goes. They act like you're disposable and incapable of resistance.

Our workplaces are undemocratic; they're hierarchical, with rules and requirements handed down from above, and almost no accountability at the top. Even though we're used to this, most people don't agree that one person at the top should have all the power, and all the "small" people at the bottom should have none.

If your co-workers feel they have no say, it's because the bosses who designed the system want to keep it that way. Our bosses almost never accommodate change from below, except when our unions force them to. They resist democracy—that is, decisions made by the majority—at all costs.

When you talk about democracy in the workplace, you are inviting your co-workers to think about how this isn't the world they want to live in. Next, you can help them see themselves as part of a group of workers. You may have little to no power individually, but you have immense power collectively.

THERE'S POWER IN OUR OWN HANDS

Just because we're treated as if we're powerless doesn't make it true. In fact, the power of working people drives the economy, society, and the world. If workers start to see this clearly, then their understanding of the balance of power in the workplace can change.

What gives us the confidence that things could be different? For some people it's studying labor history to trace the long arc of workers fighting for economic democracy in every corner of the world. You might find it worth your while to read up on the great strikes in U.S. labor history, to draw inspiration from how previous generations of ordinary workers faced down rich, powerful, and murderous employers to win the eight-hour day and bring unions into textile mills, mines, factories, slaughterhouses, and fields.

Others find their encouragement in more recent victories—like the bottom-up transformation of the Chicago Teachers Union, or the United Auto Workers strike at the Big 3 that ended two-tier wages. You might even find your source of inspiration outside of labor, in other social movements.

> The power of working people drives the economy, society, and the world.

The simplest way to help deepen this understanding, though, is to examine your own workplace. Ask your co-workers—ideally when talking in a group—what would happen if they stopped doing a particular task.

Would it disrupt production or the flow of work? Would someone else have to be called in to do it? Would it cause problems for other workers, the boss, customers, patients, students, or clients? If the answer to any of these is yes, then a conversation can start about the actual value the worker is creating.

Workers are essential. What's important is for working people to come to an understanding of their own centrality in the workplace and economy. That centrality should determine their power to control important decisions in both spheres.

THE BOSS ISN'T ALL-POWERFUL

One of the hardest jobs is helping your co-workers see that the boss is not all-powerful. Fortunately, bosses can't control our minds—though they try. As we sharpen our minds and observe how things really work, we grow more confident. We begin to trust our assessments, direct our own decisions, and choose our own actions.

Together with co-workers, try digging into the power system at your workplace or company. This can expose how productivity and profits are directed from above—and how we at the bottom can benefit by flipping that power on its head. For Kate Ziegler, it was helpful to consider what kinds of pressure the ad agencies were susceptible to, and who could bring it. Here are some questions to discuss:

- Do you know who hired your boss?
- How is the boss evaluated?
- Who directs their work?
- What are they being pressured to deliver?
- What are the different levels of management? Do they have different incentives? Are they in conflict?

Try observing your bosses not from a subordinate position but instead as equals. We are are fully capable of analyzing their behavior just as they analyze ours.

The more understanding workers gain, and the more collective self-respect they demonstrate, the more disoriented the bosses become. This shift may provoke the bosses to become even more overbearing, which can help even more workers to see their weaknesses.

CHAPTER 6: OVERCOME DIVISION AND COME TOGETHER AROUND COMMON CONCERNS

RIGHTS

Bringing a Sandwich Shop Together

As newly unionized workers prepared to strike at Seattle's Homegrown chain of sandwich shops, Kai Ortiz Sugimoto and his co-workers at the Mercer Island location had to overcome almost every conceivable kind of division among themselves.

The front-of-house workers like Ortiz, who take orders and assemble sandwiches, were mostly young. Many were high school students in this affluent suburb, or college students back for the summer.

The prep workers in the kitchen were mostly Mexican immigrants, older, with families. Many had been working difficult jobs since age 12 or 13. Prep was unrelenting, endlessly portioning meat with no real downtime, and if they finished early they would go home, which meant less pay.

Both groups had signed cards to unionize. But there wasn't yet much solidarity between them.

In the front of house, the pace ebbed and flowed with customer traffic. Prep workers saw front-of-house workers waiting idly, scrolling on their phones, finishing out slow shifts. They disapproved. Why should they stick their necks out for these workers, who also enjoyed perks and better treatment from a racist manager?

Ortiz's approach was to help out in the kitchen. He got to know prep workers—including two he recognized as leaders. Ortiz could see the prep workers' point about the difference in work ethic, but he argued it wasn't workers' job to get on each other's case. "We're not the managers," he said.

It was the discovery of a shared issue that helped bring the groups together. As the summer heated up, with no air conditioning, the temperature in the cafe was often 90 degrees and sometimes 100. Both groups suffered. Workers were getting dizzy, throwing up in the bathroom, and spending their breaks in the walk-in fridge trying to cool down. Everyone could see this was an issue worth striking over.

But there was a third group of workers at this location, catering workers, and the heat problem didn't affect them at all. They actually had air conditioning—their space had previously been the corporate office—and they were often out driving. This group had its own internal divisions along age and ethnicity lines, and one big sore point that put them at odds with the others: tips. Catering brought in big tips, which they were grudgingly obliged to split with the cafe workers.

Since workers had different shift schedules, it was tough for them to meet all together. To reach the catering workers, Ortiz interacted mostly with one key leader of the group. But among themselves, the catering workers identified their own top issue: They wanted a wage to match what drivers in the company's distribution arm were earning, since they did similar work.

> The crucial challenge was convincing everyone that they could win only by acting together.

The crucial challenge, Ortiz said, was convincing everyone that they could win only by acting together. "The boss would try to divide us the moment they saw an opportunity," he said. "When we strike, we have to do it together, not department by department—that just shows weakness, and doesn't really disrupt the whole store either." The workers decided they would all strike for both demands: air conditioning for all and the raise for catering workers.

The workers held their strike vote as a mini-strike, a test of their growing unity. Everyone walked out for five minutes to cast the vote and take a group picture. It was unanimous. But it was a bit of a bluff. Many people had voted yes just to send a message. "We knew we weren't ready to go on strike yet," Ortiz said.

Ortiz told one of the prep leaders that the two of them needed to talk outside of work. The worker hadn't been very involved yet, but "she wanted to know more," Ortiz said. "She's a really curious person." They started meeting a couple times a week at a mall, sitting down together (at a different sandwich shop chain), talking about how to overcome the divisions among Homegrown workers.

"I talked a lot about the stakes," he said. "She wants a raise for completely different reasons than my co-workers in the front. They want to save up for college or buy nice things. She wants health care for her family."

She wasn't committing to striking yet, but she started saying "maybe." It dawned on Ortiz that when she argued that "the other workers don't deserve it," something else was really holding her back: fear. And inch by inch, she was overcoming it.

The night before the strike, everyone met up at a pizzeria to confirm their commitment. One worker was still reluctant and afraid, and others were ready to give up on her. But the prep worker Ortiz had met with so many times at the mall finally convinced her. "You're not the only one who needs the money," she said. "I am taking this risk, and there's no reason why you can't do it too."

The strike began at 7:00 a.m. The catering and prep workers on shift at that time had the toughest job: walking out on their managers. Everyone else waited outside, chanting "¡Sí se puede!" ("Yes we can!") as they emerged one by one. It was the end of summer, the first day of school for the high school workers—but they showed up anyway, and spent the morning picketing before heading to class. Nobody crossed the line.

Organizing requires bringing people together around a concrete concern, deciding on goals, and taking action to accomplish them. But before moving to action, your co-workers have to see themselves as the ones who can do something about the challenges they face. It's not enough to recognize that there's a shared problem. The group has to see themselves as a group that can think and act collectively.

Unfortunately, it's no easy task to help a random group of co-workers—who have been steeped in the culture of individualism and competition—feel like an "us." It can be slow and rather discouraging, until you find your own instinctive path to unity. The ideas in this chapter will help—as will maintaining an attitude of respect, curiosity, and patience.

GETTING TO THE "US"

When you are organizing in the workplace, the "us" is workers and the "them" is the boss. It shouldn't be a very hard argument to just count heads, point out that the bosses are running things to their own advantage, and get everyone on board to flip the system—right? Ha! This depends on co-workers seeing themselves as an "us."

The employer maintains power by keeping workers divided. If they can keep us from knowing one another, trusting and supporting one another, working out our problems together, and building a stronger and stronger majority, then they've won the battle before it even starts. We have only one pathway to building a majority, and that is to overcome divisions.

Because of the unequal society we live in, workers are already divided before we walk into any job. We're divided by race and gender, by access to wealth, by education, political beliefs, religion, national origin. Add to that the competition and distrust between newer workers and those more senior, the hard workers and the slackers, and the cliques that form around job function—as well as the divide between those who are compliant with management and those who are defiant.

> The employer maintains power by keeping workers divided.

An organizer must be committed to recognizing and then looking past all divisions. Don't get discouraged or demoralized by workplace groups that may appear to hate one another. Hold tight to the belief that there is an "us" that can eventually be built despite these divisions.

DEFINE YOUR UNIVERSE

Any problem you might organize around has a universe, a group of co-workers who are affected by it—directly or indirectly—or who support those who are affected.

Choose a group of people you believe will not just agree on the problem but also be willing to take action. It could be your department with seven people—or 325. Or your entire workplace, whether it has 12 people or 3,000. Or the second shift in the B wing, or the drivers who are dispatched from 11:00 a.m. to 7:00 p.m.

The bigger the issue, the more power you'll need and the larger your group will have to be to fight and win. But if your universe is too large or ill-defined, it will be difficult to figure out what people are willing to do and to work through their fears.

In general, it's better to build up from small to large. If the issue you want to address is huge, see if you can find a smaller, winnable fight to start with. Once you show that something can be done, more becomes possible.

Here's an example of a well-defined universe: Nurses in a short-staffed hospital emergency department were continually asked to take extra shifts. Under their contract, overtime was voluntary—but nurses typically accepted it because they worried that if they didn't, the hospital would expand its use of nonunion agency nurses to fill the gaps.

Members talked it over and agreed that for a week they would all refuse overtime. Eighty-five percent participated. Management couldn't fill that many gaps with agency nurses all at once, and was desperate to bring the overtime boycott to an end—so it was forced to start hiring more nurses.

Short staffing wasn't just a problem in the emergency department; it was a hospital-wide problem affecting thousands of workers. The union had been trying to address the issue in bargaining for years, and hadn't made any headway.

But by tackling the problem in one department where nurses all knew and trusted each other, workers were able to take action and score a win. That win set an example that other departments could follow and build on.

To achieve the unity needed for effective action, a group should usually be defined by some yardstick of the workplace (like everyone in a particular department or job), not by an "in-crowd."

See if you can find a smaller, winnable fight to start with.

If your workplace feels divided into groups that mistrust one another, it's especially helpful to reach across the aisle and connect with other workers who are not like you—as Kai Ortiz did when he reached out to the kitchen prep workers. Consider when, where, and how you can meet up. It may be uncomfortable and hard to find shared concerns, but this is the direction you need to move if you're going to build power.

WORK THROUGH MISUNDERSTANDINGS

Before you can open up dialogue between people, you may need to address misunderstandings that could get in the way.

In an Amazon warehouse, a few workers were trying to pull together an organizing committee, but suspicions among different groups—Haitians, Algerians, weed smokers, and a "discombobulated" morning shift group—kept slowing any progress.

Finally, someone named it: "Those Haitians can't be trusted." Why not? "They're in the manager's pocket." Why do you say that? "Because they do anything he says. They grab all the overtime they can get."

The workers who were trying to organize talked with some friends among the Haitian workers. They learned that these new immigrants were sending home as much of their wages as possible to support desperately poor and displaced family members in Haiti.

Helping their co-workers understand this context eased tensions. A few weeks later, when the organizing committee put on a barbecue, socializing across the groups was much more relaxed.

NOTICE COMMON CONCERNS AND TEST THEM

The first step in building up a group is having thoughtful one-on-one conversations, like those described in chapter 1. One-on-one conversations are especially useful in this early stage because some people may be shy about sharing more widely, worried about stirring up trouble, or distrustful of their co-workers.

If you keep a fresh and curious ear, you may start to notice some common threads in your conversations. You're talking to your fifth co-worker in this hospital cafeteria, and you keep hearing that it's hard to cook enough food on schedule because important pieces of equipment are in disrepair. Management has been told, but nothing's been done.

So you may try to test how widely shared this concern is: "We've all noticed that three of the four ovens haven't been working for the past six months. There are also problems with the automatic slicer. What do you think about that? I know how it affects me, but how does it affect you? How has it changed your work? Do you know if anyone has tried to get this addressed? What do you think should be done about it?"

Be open to the possibility that you're on the wrong track—it may be that only a small number of workers care about this problem. Or maybe other problems are more urgent. Keep sounding people out until you're pretty confident that they are willing to sit down with others.

BRING PEOPLE INTO GROUP DISCUSSIONS

Individual conversations are just a bridge to group dialogue.

Remember that individual conversations are just a bridge to group dialogue. That could be inviting five people to sit around the break table. It could be a Zoom meeting you've taken weeks to set up that will have 30 people on it. It could be going out for beer on Friday night because things have reached a breaking point and you've gotten people to see that we need to talk about it.

Whatever the setting, it's in the give and take of group discussion that the confidence, clarity, and courage needed for collective action emerge. When people are invited to listen to each other in a respectful environment, they have a chance to hear other people's experience, get a sense of shared purpose, and overcome fears of taking action. It can be transformative.

Even getting people to just sit down together may require some work. You are likely to hear that they have no time, that they don't see the point because nothing will change, or that they don't want a target on their back.

Take these objections as starting points for conversation. The best way to ease those concerns is by showing respect, listening, and offering encouragement. There's no need to argue, and in fact it won't help.

Just keep inviting them to talk.

You may need to reassure someone that a group discussion isn't a commitment to join something, but rather a chance to share experience, ideas, and insights. If they do come and the tone is good, the attitude is respectful, and they don't feel pressured, then they may come back. At some point later, you can ask them to reflect: *How was that? Useful? Interesting? Different from what you expected?*

Helping people feel welcome in meetings is essential to creating a group identity, and a necessary building block to powerful organizing.

A FEELING OF IDENTITY

When you have slowly and carefully knitted the group together based on shared recognition and respect, it then becomes more possible to plan and take action together. Before moving forward, reflect on how you've gotten this far.

Hopefully your group—including people across differences of race, age, and national origin—has now started to see itself as *a group*. You might notice some changes: People seem more relaxed, they're listening to each other better, or they've traded complaining for constructive brainstorming.

Point out what you've noticed and ask your co-workers, "What do you think—how are we doing as a group?" If people say things like "It feels good," "I'm surprised," "I always thought we could do this, we just never did," or "It's great to look around and see we have so many things in common," then you're becoming a group that can take action together.

If people feel more confident, if they feel that those around them are allies, that you share something together—then you've already begun to change the balance of power. People aren't bickering; they're taking coffee breaks together. The feeling of tension and distrust among co-workers starts to be replaced by friendliness, consideration, and respect.

The next step, taking action together, can bring people together in an even deeper way.

CHAPTER 7: OVERCOME FEAR AND TAKE COLLECTIVE ACTION

DAE
DAE

School Sickouts Build the Union

When the school district in Durham, North Carolina, decided to claw back a long-overdue raise from 1,500 of its lowest-paid "classified staff" workers, wildcat strikes broke out.

The actions were scattered but bold. "In one school the entire cafeteria staff didn't show up," said social studies teacher Carlos Perez. A handful of custodians and front office staff stayed home too.

At the time, the Durham Association of Educators (DAE) was in the middle of a year-long campaign to get a majority of the district's 5,000 teachers and classified staff to join the union. Members were tabling in school parking lots and visiting bus barns, asking people to join. By the time the "Classified Staff Pay Debacle" hit, 800 workers had signed up.

When the wildcat actions started, the union "rose to the occasion," Perez said. Members decided to see if they could fan the flames of spontaneous action into an organized campaign that could move the school board.

On short notice, 100 workers showed up to a mass meeting and settled on demands. "We organized a rally thinking we would get 500 people," Perez said, "and 1,000 showed up. Organizing committees started up in different schools and grew rapidly."

The union decided to escalate to rolling sickouts. But even though the anger was widespread, "not all schools were immediately able to pull off an organized work stoppage," Perez said. "So we started to build capacity." The union asked workers to sign "action cards" that committed them to specific actions they'd take if the district didn't respond to the union's demands.

Members in each school talked about what percentage of workers would need to commit before they took action: 90 percent? 75 percent? "We agreed you needed to talk to every worker in the building," Perez said. At Jordan High School, where he works, 85 percent committed.

It helped that Jordan already had a workplace committee that for years had emphasized building relationships with all workers in the school, not just teachers. In Durham, the classified staff are disproportionately Black or Latino, while many of the teachers are white. The union battles a perception that it is just a "teachers union."

Members set out to fan the flames of spontaneous action into an organized campaign.

"We have tried to be consistent, follow through and really throw down," Perez said. Organizers have been thoughtful about when meetings are scheduled, and offer food and childcare so it's easier to participate. "And we had classified staff in leadership positions," Perez said. "This makes a difference. We bring you in, share information, and help you become involved." Over time, workers see that getting active can make a difference in their lives.

"I remember the night we were trying to get commitments for the sickout the next day," said Perez. "I called someone on the front office staff, a middle-aged Black woman, and she said, 'A lot of people are saying DAE is the bomb.' This told me people knew we were really taking it seriously."

The first sickout was on a Thursday and included 12 of the district's 56 schools. Among them were some of the biggest schools, including Jordan, with 180 workers and 2,000 students. "The district feels that," Perez said. "We agreed that after the initial pickets at our own schools, we'd send a team to another school at the end of the day to talk to workers as they were leaving, explaining why we were doing it and what the issues were."

The school board met that Friday and agreed to some of the union's demands. On Saturday, the campaign's district-wide coordinating committee met and debated whether to stop the rolling sickouts or keep going. Another round of schools was already preparing to go out on Monday.

At first the committee members proposed to halt the action. But "there was grumbling," Perez said. "A number of classified staff walked out in opposition."

At the meeting, everyone was sitting at tables with others from their own school. "I started walking around to those tables, asking what people were thinking," Perez said. Those who were dissatisfied felt the union needed to send a clearer message to the school board—"*This is what you need to do to stop the sickouts*"—and hold out for a commitment on the budget.

"It was a moment when we really could have lost trust" with the classified workers, Perez said. "It had been years of disrespect from the union. Then they finally got a big raise, then it was taken back. They finally took militant action, and now it was being stopped. I said, 'If it comes down to maintaining a good relationship with the school board or standing with our co-workers, we'll do that every time.'"

Seven more schools struck on Monday. Then the school board met all the union's demands.

It was, said Perez, "the biggest budget increase they'd ever made." And the cherry on top: The union reached majority membership, too.

"Standing in solidarity with classified staff really helped," Perez said. "At a certain point, we realized we needed a lot more cards to meet the deadline" and that "we had lots more people who had developed during the campaign, who were excited to be part of a movement, and were eager to get those last cards."

It's not enough to just bring people together to talk. We have to take collective action to fix problems and challenge the boss's absolute control of the workplace.

This is something that a group of workers can do at almost any time, in almost any workplace. You don't need permission, legal authority, or a big and powerful union. You just need to decide to do something collectively to try and solve a problem and achieve a goal you all share.

Most of us have a habit of expecting that problems can only be solved from above. It's deeply ingrained in us. When there's any kind of problem, we tend to either suck it up and suffer in silence, or complain but decline to do anything about it.

Possibly we will go tell the boss, hoping he'll fix it. Maybe, if it's bad enough, we'll try to file a grievance or get a lawyer. Of course filing grievances and unfair labor practice charges can be helpful. But we shouldn't only rely on people above us, like the courts or H.R., to fix problems. We should learn how to fix them ourselves, together.

DECIDE TOGETHER WHAT TO DO

A plan handed down from above by union officers or staffers may be strategically brilliant. But if the members who are called into action haven't had the chance to shape the plan and endorse it, it may well be flawed and uninspiring. A directive from someone higher up, even a union officer, still reflects the boss's culture, which we don't want to replicate. If we are serious about building power democratically, it has to start here.

To act collectively, the people affected by the problem need to discuss what to do. They may arrive at a plan that includes individual action—for instance, identifying a spokesperson for a delegation—but what makes it collective is that it was decided together.

To act collectively, the people affected by the problem need to discuss what to do.

Even if a collectively agreed-on action doesn't contribute to winning something concrete on the issue, it may be valuable in other ways—for instance, it increases the group's confidence and sense of solidarity, and helps protect an individual or a group of workers.

WHO GETS THINGS GOING?

There's a bullseye target on the cover of the Labor Notes book *Secrets of a Successful Organizer*. It's a reminder that on any issue, some group in the workforce will tend to feel more engaged than others. They are at the center of the bullseye. They are the ones who can get things going.

The members of this group—those who are most concerned about or feel most affected by the issue, or are most willing to participate—will change over time.

If you are standing at the center of the circles, are you constantly looking for the most motivated people in the next circle out, and inviting them in? Open the door. Invite the next person in, and the next, and the next. Ask them who else they know who could be engaged in tackling workplace problems.

The core group should always be expanding.

AIM FOR THE BULLSEYE

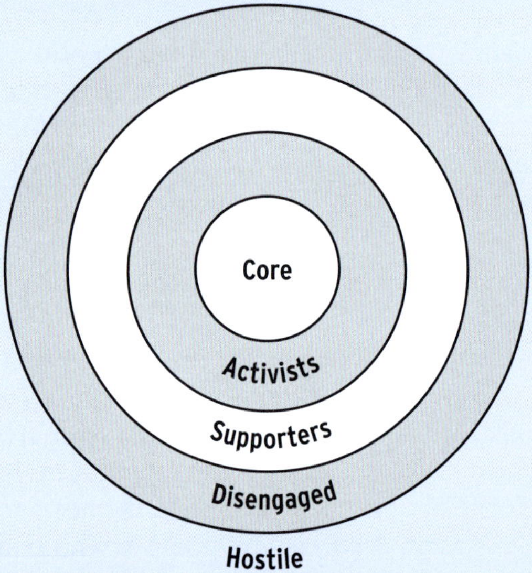

- **Core group:** These people are always thinking about organizing and how to get others involved, even on their time off. They might be elected leaders or shop stewards, or not.
- **Activists:** These people can be counted on to help when an issue heats up. They will take responsibility to get the word out and will ask other people to take action, too.
- **Supporters:** These people will wear a button or sign a petition, but don't take

responsibility for getting anyone else involved.

- **Disengaged:** These people don't see the union as a factor in their lives, so they don't participate.
- **Hostile:** There are also people outside the circle who aren't just uninvolved—they're hostile to the union. Don't waste your time arguing with the haters. Maybe one day something will open their eyes, but it'll probably be an experience, not a debate, that does it.

—*Secrets of a Successful Organizer*

If the process becomes static, and it's always the same group of people carrying out the work, this is something to look at and try to solve. Because when that inner group gets too small and too stable, the tendency will be to make decisions on behalf of the whole group, rather than continually consulting the larger group.

Organizers should help their fellow workers brainstorm ideas, assess what's realistic, think things through step by step, and decide on a plan. You can point out possible opportunities or pitfalls, ask questions to flush out potential weaknesses in the planning, and offer technical or legal information if you have it. Of course you can state your own opinion too! But your main job is to respect and elevate the process among the whole group, to help support it but never dominate it.

DON'T TAKE ACTION WITHOUT SETTING GOALS FIRST

Before you can take any action, you have to define goals, as classified staff in Durham schools did in Carlos Perez's story. Their goal: a raise. After the first sickout, when they won a partial victory, the group threatened to fracture. Democratic dialogue was needed to get everyone back on the same page about their goals from that point forward.

There may be multiple possible goals, and the specifics matter. Take the example of the hospital cafeteria workers discussed in the previous chapter. They might ask: Is our only goal to get the ovens repaired? Replaced? Do we want to make sure that they're replaced whenever one of them is not working well, or be assured that we can adjust the menu so that we won't need an oven so much? Do we want a direct relationship with the guy in maintenance who can fix the oven? Do we think the real problem is that the wiring is ancient, and what we need is a comprehensive electrical reboot?

Treat your fellow workers as the experts.

Treat your fellow workers as the experts. Your job is to elicit as much thinking as you possibly can, because it builds people's self-confidence and respect for one another when they listen to one another's ideas in a dignified environment.

Some ideas may be sensible, some not. Some goals may just not be winnable, at least until the group has built more power. But you'll see the members of the group start to behave with more and more flexibility and respect toward one another as you model this. Then a few goals will emerge.

RANK YOUR GOALS AND ACTIONS, COLLECTIVELY

Most workplace problems will contain smaller and larger goals. If you've collectively arrived at three or four goals, you might ask people: Should any of these be achieved before others? Or are some more likely to be achieved? Invite people to try and place them in some kind of order, to create a logical sequence.

An organizer gets good at summarizing and checking: "OK, we've agreed that there are three stoves not working. B and C seem to mostly work except if we're using them continuously more than four hours at a time. People seem to agree that stove A has to be replaced. For stoves B and C, management just has to allow us to build our baking schedule. Does that sound right?"

But then other smaller goals pop up. Someone might say that the kitchen budget has been flatlined for years and there's no money for a new stove. You might ask if that's just hearsay or if they've seen the budget. Who is familiar with the budget? How can we get a copy?

Each of these small goals can lead to action. If Lucille knows she can talk to her brother-in-law about the hospital budget on Saturday, and then you can all meet again with info she got, you're all going to feel like you've taken a step out of powerlessness. That's an incredibly helpful part of the organizing process.

TAKING BOTTOM-UP ACTION CHANGES THE BALANCE OF POWER

There are different ways a union can take action to solve problems. A top-down approach may solve the immediate workplace problem, but it may not change the balance of power. Engaging as many members as possible in a bottom-up approach may accomplish both goals.

For example, consider how things might play out after the boss unilaterally announces an unpopular new schedule. Things are likely to go differently depending on which approach you take, top-down vs. bottom-up:

Timeline	Top-Down Action	Bottom-Up Action
Week 1	The boss unilaterally announces a new work schedule. The union president talks to the boss. The boss holds firm on the schedule.	The boss unilaterally announces a new work schedule. Members affected by the proposed schedule change start talking, complaining, and meeting with stewards to brainstorm a response.

Timeline	Top-Down Action	Bottom-Up Action
	The president sends a message to members saying the union will file a request to bargain the impact of the new schedule.	The president sends a message to members saying the union will file a request to bargain the impact of the new schedule. Ten-minute meetings are organized throughout the workplace to discuss the new schedule. Lots of questions and complaints surface.
Week 2	No response from the boss on the request to bargain.	No response from the boss on the request to bargain, but managers and supervisors seem alarmed by the workplace meetings. Stewards, grievance reps, and board members meet to compile complaints and generate answers to questions. The president writes to members summarizing the shared concerns and calling a general meeting. Stewards post notices about the general meeting and talk to co-workers to encourage attendance.

Timeline	Top-Down Action	Bottom-Up Action
Week 3	No response from the boss on the request to bargain.	At the general meeting, participants adopt a plan to conduct face-to-face survey meetings to collate objections to the new schedule and possible alternatives. Survey meetings are scheduled. The president announces the survey meetings, with time and place. Stewards post notices about the survey meetings and talk to co-workers to encourage attendance.
Week 4	No response from the boss on the request to bargain. A grievance is filed.	No response from the boss on the request to bargain. A grievance is filed. Survey meetings are held and results compiled. The president seeks volunteers for a committee to draft an alternative schedule. The committee meets and issues a proposed alternative schedule, distributed to all members for discussion. Revisions are made.

Timeline	Top-Down Action	Bottom-Up Action
Week 5	No response to the grievance.	The president calls a general meeting to review and adopt the alternative schedule.
	The president sends a communication saying a grievance is in process.	The alternative schedule is printed in petition form and distributed for members to sign on.
		The alternative schedule is presented to the boss by a large delegation of members.
Week 6	The boss imposes the new schedule.	The boss unilaterally issues an improved schedule which reflects some compromise.
	Individual grievances are filed for affected members.	The president calls a meeting for members to discuss and vote on the compromise schedule. It is rejected by the members.
Weeks 6-12	Grievances languish.	The president proposes an open meeting with the boss to make improvements on the schedule. Silence from the boss.
Week 13	Grievances are denied and sent to arbitration.	Members begin wearing stickers: *Let's Talk or We Walk.*

Timeline	Top-Down Action	Bottom-Up Action
Week 27	Arbitration is scheduled.	The boss agrees to meet, but only with the president. The president declines to meet privately.
Week 34	Arbitration is held.	The boss meets with a "Schedule Bargaining Team" and many members attend as observers. An improved compromise schedule is reached.
Week 37	Grievances are denied. The new schedule is retained.	The members meet, discuss, and vote to ratify the new schedule, and they feel powerful!

At first the approach on the left might appear forceful—immediate action is taken by the president. But a request to bargain is an action that the boss knows how to ignore. The longer it drags on, the more disaffected the members become.

By taking their time and talking among themselves in a well-organized way, the members of the union on the right not only involve everyone and develop a comprehensive demand, but also make their demand very difficult for the boss to ignore or refuse. And in the process, they strengthen connections and build power.

HEY, ISN'T THIS ILLEGAL?

Most workers feel that they have no power themselves, and that the only real power that could force their boss to fix a problem is provided by the contract, or a policy, or a law. But no law assisted the classified staff in the Durham schools to win their raises back—in fact, public sector collective bargaining is illegal in North Carolina.

Laws, policies, and the contract do matter. Of course a good union will educate members about the rights and protections they afford, and how stewards, grievance reps, and lawyers work to enforce those rights through administrative and legal means.

But this approach rarely changes the balance of power between labor and management. Building power requires bringing workers together to take action against the boss, not turning the problem over to someone else to fix.

This way of thinking may be unfamiliar to your co-workers. It's no surprise that most want a rep or lawyer to "take their case." Our labor movement has become more like an insurance company, where members pay dues to get protection in case something bad happens.

The bosses don't want us to feel that there's anything we can do on our own. They would prefer a system where workers have no rights at all. But if a union does exist, they want it to be as tame and compliant as possible. A grievance system that relies on professional union staff talking to Human Resources staff is pretty tame.

Building power requires bringing workers together to take action against the boss.

Generally speaking, the boss has the upper hand in such processes. They have more lawyers than we do, and whole layers of middle managers to deflect conflict. Delay works in their favor, and they can achieve it by missing deadlines, ignoring information requests, and filing endless appeals. All the while, our aggrieved members are growing more frustrated and angry—at the union—for failing to fix their problem. A double benefit to the boss.

For all these reasons, employers are happy to keep things at a bureaucratic or legal level. We shouldn't let our unions get trapped there. Of course it is useful at times to pursue grievances and arbitration. But the heart of organizing is workers taking direct collective action to solve problems.

DIRECT ACTION TAKES TRUST

As everybody who has worked under a union contract knows, the moment the contract is signed the employer will be trying to evade it, undermine it, reinterpret it, and not give you what you thought you won. So unity is important when we're trying to win a contract, but it's just as important once we've won it. Then, we need day-to-day unity. If we're not unified and motivated to protect what we've won, we will lose it.

A shop steward in a letter carriers union was barely clinging to his sanity. "I file, on average, 17 grievances a week," he reported. Almost all of them were over a certain kind of mandated overtime that very clearly violated the contract—yet management kept doing it every day. Hundreds of grievances had not stopped the practice. Going over the boss's head to the regional postmaster had not stopped it.

After talking with a union mentor, the steward decided to try helping his co-workers get comfortable policing their overtime rights from below. They talked it over and agreed that if anybody saw anybody else being mandated, they would get a few co-workers together and go over to the boss and say, "We're not going to take it."

It worked. Once they felt like part of a team effort, people got some courage and started refusing the mandated overtime—they just told the supervisor they were clocking out. The backlog of work started causing ripples at the regional office, and the supervisor was moved to a different post office. Some part-timers were brought on full-time and the workload became manageable without endless overtime.

Enforcement from below is the most effective way to defend our contractual rights. It's also how you change the culture of the workplace. The boss can withstand grievances, but not this.

Enforcement from below is the most effective way to defend our contractual rights.

But to do it, you need people who are willing to actually take action as it's happening, in real time. You need to trust each other, because it's risky. Over time you and your co-workers can develop a commitment to one another. You expect to be treated with integrity, and you know you can rely on each other to stand up for it together.

BUT WHAT ACTION TO TAKE?

This chapter has focused on helping co-workers get ready to take powerful collective action. For ideas of specific actions, and guidance on how to build a campaign of escalating actions, check out the book *Secrets of a Successful Organizer* and numerous organizing guides produced by unions.

The focus of this book is the relationships, trust, dialogue, and decision-making practice needed to keep going for the long haul.

Once a group feels solid enough to commit to a collective action of any sort—whether it's writing a letter, wearing pins, showing up for a group confrontation with a boss, or even a strike—consider these three criteria for a successful action:

1. Does this action have the potential to shift the balance of power and win improvements that people are seeking?
2. Has everyone involved considered the risks and are they ready to take them?
3. Will this action build the power and capacity of the union (or the group, or the caucus)?

If an action meets these tests, give it a try and keep going!

CHAPTER 8: REFLECT ON THE CHANGING BALANCE OF POWER AND KEEP GOING

How Volkswagen Workers Rose from the Ashes

Workers at the Volkswagen plant in Chattanooga, Tennessee, started organizing in 2014 to join the United Auto Workers. They lost two elections before finally winning a decade later, on their third try.

Yolanda Peoples hired in at the plant when it first opened. She came from a UAW family and was always pro-union. Still, she "stayed in the background" of the first union drive. "I didn't want to rock the boat too much," she said.

Despite VW's official stance of neutrality, many supervisors were anti-union. Workers had a justified fear of being disciplined for discussing the union on the job. So union supporters were "real hush-hush—we were like a secret society," Peoples said.

In this climate of fear, it was hard to counter the barrage of vote-no talking points from Tennessee politicians, major media, and national anti-union groups.

"We rushed it," Peoples said. The union lost the vote.

In the aftermath, she said, some union supporters were targeted; others got the message to keep their heads down. And despite the company's promises, "absolutely nothing changed," Peoples said.

In the next attempt, in 2019, she decided to get more involved. This time workers knew what to expect, and Peoples felt the momentum was on their side—until management brought in two anti-union guest speakers: the governor of Tennessee and a popular former CEO, Frank Fischer.

Fischer pleaded with workers to "give VW one more chance," Peoples said. "He was so heartfelt. That destroyed us." The union lost narrowly. And of course, "Frank Fischer got on his plane and we never heard from him again."

It was painful to watch management exploit workers' trust with empty promises, Peoples said. "But in the long run it helped, because we knew it was something they could not try again."

It was painful to watch management exploit workers' trust with empty promises.

The volunteer organizing committee felt devastated and burnt out after their second loss. But the members had grown very close during those two drives. They still chatted every day when they ran into each other. That's how conversations started in 2023 about making another run at organizing—at just the time when the UAW's contract campaign at the Big 3 automakers was making waves.

Peoples was all-in this time: loud and clear, pro-union,

no fear. After all these years, people knew where she stood and came to her for advice. She wanted to use her influence. It felt like now or never.

This time the volunteer organizing committee got better advice from the UAW: If they were allowed to talk about their families and the ball game while working, they had a legal right to talk about the union too.

They decided to put these on-the-job conversations at the heart of their campaign—building the union with people they knew and trusted. "We're working beside these people eight to 12 hours a day," Peoples said. "We see the people we work beside probably more than we see our families."

She made it her mission to talk with at least one new person per week.

She also made it her mission to talk with at least one new person per week. She found this opened the door to many new friendships, sometimes with people she had walked past for 13 years. "I have heard so many stories where I just could not believe the things they've gone through," she said.

The committee grew to 200 members, including two from every line. The union won the vote in a blowout: 2,628 to 985.

Two days later, the first union meeting was packed wall to wall. "Everybody wanted to know what's the next step," Peoples said. "Everybody wanted to get involved." An election committee was formed for the bargaining team. The organizing committee kept co-workers in touch with the process.

Peoples reflected afterward that the losses had taught critical lessons. "Without those two fails we would not have been equipped enough to see past all the anti-union nonsense," she said.

Workers had learned what to expect from the company, and how they would have to prepare. They learned what kinds of conversations and communication networks they would need.

They learned to analyze how the plant was changing and recognize when conditions were ripe for another try. And they got to know themselves, and each other, as organizers—laying a strong foundation for their new union.

The goal of organizing is to change the balance of power. Organizers help co-workers reflect and keep going with this long-term goal in mind. Without reflection, we might get caught up in immediate fights and fail to see the forest for the trees.

It is through reflection that we gain perspective, learn lessons from what we tried, and steady ourselves to keep at it.

What is the balance of power? In a typical workplace, every important decision is in the hands of the boss. We want to claw back as much of that power as possible so that the workplace can be more decent, dignified, and democratic. Since the only way to change the balance of power is to turn more and more members into organizers, we must investigate how people change.

Changing the balance of power is different from winning a specific demand. There will always be new problems arising, new fights to be had. If we've actually shifted the balance of power, we've changed something about ourselves, collectively. And it's something we maintain, so we will be starting the next fight from a stronger place.

GO BEYOND "WHAT DID WE WIN?"

Evaluations of campaigns tend to begin and end with "What did we win (or not win)?" That's important but it doesn't give members a real look into *how* this was accomplished.

Your co-workers might think a good result is about the skill and cunning of the union leaders, or the feebleness of the boss—or the reverse, if the outcome is bad. Or a win might be interpreted as good luck, or a combination of economic factors beyond anyone's control. And of course these factors are real, as they were at Volkswagen.

The point of reflecting, though, is to learn from our own experience what we ourselves can change, and how we can change things in a way that builds our collective power for the long term.

> Acknowledge the outcome, but don't put all your focus on it.

Acknowledge the outcome, but don't put all your focus on it. Focus more on the process.

QUESTIONS FOR REFLECTION

Reflection should be something that happens throughout an organizing campaign—so that you're always building and adjusting, building and adjusting, building and adjusting.

Whenever you come to the natural conclusion of a campaign that your group has organized—no matter whether you won or lost—plan a debrief conversation. The point is not only to draw lessons (this worked well, that was a mistake) but also to assess the new state of play: How have people's thinking, attitudes, and relationships changed?

Discuss questions like these:

- Think about a co-worker you had a chance to observe during this campaign. Did you learn something about them that surprised you? Did you see them change? How and why did they change?
- What were the most valuable things you observed co-workers contributing to the union's work during this campaign?
- Did you have the chance to encourage or advise co-workers during the campaign? If so, what did you do? Was it effective? Could this dynamic continue?
- Did you observe some change in your own attitudes or ideas? Was the change helpful?

- Were there some things you didn't want to do at first? Did that change? Why?
- Were you or your co-workers ever scared? How about cynical, disengaged, critical, or hopeless? Did that change? How did you manage these emotions—and other obstacles?
- Did your level of trust toward anyone else in the union change during the course of the campaign, for better or for worse? What were the factors in building or breaking down trust? Did you learn something about how trust can be built?

Yolanda Peoples, for instance, overcame a great deal of fear—first her own, then her co-workers'—in the first two union drives. She and the other committee members weren't starting from scratch in the third go-round. They had gotten a lot of practice talking with co-workers about the union, and had developed a trusted core group across the plant.

A CAUCUS CAN HOLD ITS OWN DEBRIEF

If you are in a reform caucus that's trying to democratize the union, consider holding your own debrief after a campaign that was led by union officers. In addition to the above, you could ask:

- How was the campaign initiated, and how did members react? Were they curious, enthusiastic, indifferent, scared, or resistant?
- When the union officers took action, was it in the open or behind closed doors?
- Were there opportunities for members to get involved? If they got involved, what were the results?
- Was the issue resolved? What was the feeling we were left with?
- What might be the next steps?

ARE WE HELPING MORE PEOPLE BECOME ORGANIZERS?

Often union members, when faced with a problem, will automatically think, "That's for my building rep to do"—or for my steward, communications team, or the union lawyer to do.

All these people may be helpful, but they may be stretched thin. There will never be a budget big enough to hire all the people needed to do the work that could be done by members who are engaged organizers.

The UAW could never have sent 200 organizers to the Volkswagen plant. And even if it did, they wouldn't have had the impact of 200 volunteer organizers like Yolanda Peoples talking union with the people they work alongside day after day.

The familiar ideas about how to expand union capacity—more staff, a bigger budget, more swag, better contact lists, an impressive website, a snappy social media presence—miss the point. Here's what it means to increase the union's capacity: *Enable more of our co-workers to become organizers.* Devote attention, resources, and time to increasing workers' participation and build skills, analytic abilities, courage, and resilience.

> Devote attention, resources, and time to increasing workers' participation.

Resources like staff time could be deployed to help support that goal. But we don't necessarily have control over the revenue, budget, or staffing of our unions. And even if the union does have a big staff, the leaders may not want to use them in the way that the members think they should be used. Ultimately, what members can control is their own willingness to act collectively.

KEEP GOING!

To keep going means to not give up your *intention* to build power collectively. There will be many times when you or your co-workers are exhausted, despairing, or just very confused about what to do next—as the Volkswagen organizers felt after their devastating losses. That's normal. But that's no reason to abandon your intention to keep building power collectively.

Sometimes, in a weakened state, it's hard to imagine doing anything. Hopelessness puts its hooks in us.

But the basic rule for organizers is that we know there is always something that can be done to alter the balance of power. There are always some steps to take. Small steps are still steps. A small group is still a group. Small shifts in power are still shifts. And they can all accumulate.

Helping your co-workers keep going is not cheerleading, exhortation, pressure, or raising false hopes. We shouldn't strive to convince people of a reality they don't believe. Of course people are skeptical when they think they're being sold something. (Also, if you're selling something and somebody buys it, they will hold you responsible if it doesn't work.)

Instead, invite your co-workers to learn from their own experiences. When someone wants to give up, listen to them. Listen for the underlying conviction, the commitment to the values that brought them into organizing in the first place. Invite them to remember other times when things turned to ash and then, somehow, a flame was rekindled. Help them recall what led to other "reboots" in their lives.

There is always something that can be done to alter the balance of power.

Invite them to consider that brutal self-criticism might not help as much as remembering those moments of resilience. There's a difference between learning from what went wrong and beating ourselves up so much that we can't bring ourselves to make eye contact.

There will certainly be times when you, as an organizer, will wonder if *you* can keep going. At those times, it's fine to step back for a little break. Get some sleep or exercise or take time with friends. Talk to a mentor or comrade who is not deeply involved in your current campaigns. But keep a clear commitment in the back of your mind: You are still in the fight. You're just catching your breath.

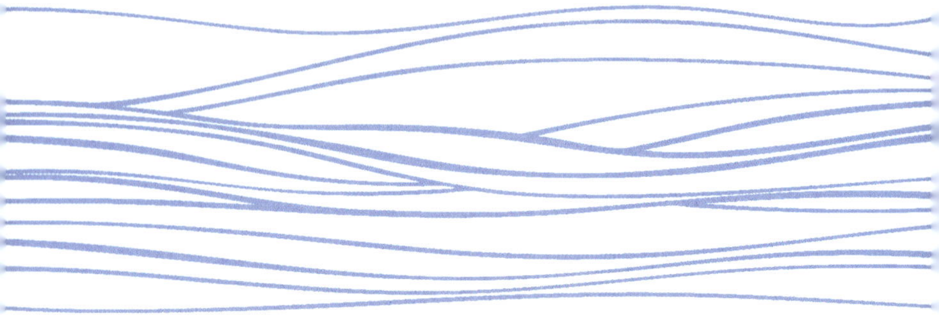

PART III: GETTING UNSTUCK

Getting stuck from time to time—and then unstuck—is just part of an organizer's hard work. This section of the book will help you figure out how to get unstuck.

The first step is not to get destabilized. Don't let frustration, fear, self-doubt, or hopelessness get their claws into you. Keep a steady eye on your goal. In the process of evaluating what's got you stuck and what remedies could work, you'll grow as an organizer—and if you troubleshoot together, you'll help others to grow as well.

Here are some places where organizers often get stuck, with suggestions for how to apply the principles and ingredients discussed in chapters 1–8 to these situations.

Apathy

If you were to poll union activists at all levels, you would get an incredible consensus that member apathy is a problem. The same questions come up frequently: "How do we get more people to participate? How do we convince people to come to meetings? How do we deal with apathy?"

Many members who are unhappy about something on the job will start under a dark cloud of despair—because they believe that most of their co-workers just don't care. If that is your starting point, your work will be much harder. If you believe in your heart that union members don't care about improving their own lives, you've already declared defeat.

It may be helpful to think of apathy as a disguise. The person who *appears* apathetic may be feeling frightened, hopeless, or angry. Or maybe no one's ever approached them before to suggest developing a plan of action. It's likely they *do* care about problems on the job, but have no idea what to do about them. They may have tried 20 times to make things better and given up. Apathy can be a convenient all-purpose mask to wear when you just don't want things to get worse.

It may be helpful to think of apathy as a disguise.

If someone's apathy is actually just resignation, you may be able to restore their hope bit by bit by sharing union victories that you care about. It might be a small win in your workplace, or a big one, like the Stand-Up Strike of 2023, when the United Auto Workers roared back from decades of complacency and won record wage increases. You don't need to exhort, just offer up real instances when something was accomplished against the odds.

Apathy is reduced almost magically by being in a group of supportive co-workers.

Apathy is reduced almost magically by being in a group of supportive co-workers. Hearing them talk, feeling stirrings of familiarity, people will inevitably relax their guard a bit and begin to feel a greater sense of safety and inclusion.

Don't start with meetings—especially if that looks *boring*, or like more work. Instead, try something fun and convivial. Maybe you're the person who brings doughnuts every Friday morning, and gets to your station early enough so others can stop by to chat. Possibly it's an informal barbecue after work, or a game of pickup basketball in the park, or sharing cake on someone's birthday. Over time, you can normalize "union talk" outside of meetings. Ask about problems at work, share what you know about union activities, or ask for input on something the union is working on. You may draw in some people who hate meetings but will get interested if they're included in informal ways.

Some UPS Teamsters in California started having "Unity Breakfasts" at a local coffee shop every Friday. At first it was just a couple of members, but they were having a good time connecting, and word spread. It naturally evolved into a strong network to support a contract campaign and possible strike.

Another great antidote to apathy is being valued and needed. Try to discover what your co-worker is good at: Someone who spends time on social media may have suggestions for upping the union's presence. An artist could design a logo for the union letterhead or T-shirt. Some people are good at meeting new people and could be great on the new member orientation team. Don't ask them to take on union tasks that you want done; instead help them think about what they have to contribute that's meaningful to them. Your job as an organizer is to fit that contribution into what the union is doing. Respect can chase apathy away.

Fear

What's the greatest gift the labor movement offers? It's not the ability to bargain a contract, protect yourself on the job, or win higher wages, though those are important.

The greatest gift is a path out of fear. Once we can see that path under our feet, the real fightback and movement-building can begin.

A workplace organizer has to help their co-workers find the path out of fear.

In many workplaces, it feels like fear is saturating us. Ask a co-worker how things are going, and the complaints will pour forth. But invite that same co-worker to attend a small meeting, join with others and talk to the boss, sign a petition, or defend a co-worker who's being bullied—and fear comes up like a brick wall. Fear of retaliation, of losing "access" to a boss, of creating division, of losing friends, of losing a job, of being labeled a complainer or a troublemaker.

This fear seems so normal that most people don't question it. In fact, they will question *you*, the person bringing this trouble to them. And so we stumble along, isolated, accepting fear and misery as if they were inevitable. This culture of fear serves bosses very well. They know that workers are grumbling, but as long as the grumbling doesn't turn into action, they can disregard it.

A workplace organizer has to help their co-workers find the path out of fear. Don't blame, judge, or dismiss people for being fearful—help them get through it. This may be a long and uneven process. Your patience will be key.

Here's what unions *can't* do to alleviate fear: We can't tout the power of labor laws, which are mostly too weak to offer reassuring protection. We can't promise that someone else—union officers, government agencies—will do the heavy lifting. We can't deny that there are risks to taking action. And we can't make guarantees. Results are conditioned on how much power we build.

Instead, start with your own attitude. Are you ready to trust your co-workers, even if your workplace has longstanding divisions? Cultivate a sense of curiosity about them. Bring respect—if not for their beliefs, then for the contribution they can make.

Banish cynicism. It has no place in organizing. Radiate confidence that you, collectively, can shift the balance of power. Inspire your co-worker to feel: "At last, someone is listening to me! I'm not invisible."

Fear is reduced by steady conversation—one on one, in small groups, in big groups. The more we hear other people's experiences and recognize commonalities, the less isolated we become. Every development in the workplace, every attempted fightback, every counter-move by the boss, should trigger purposeful conversation.

> **Fear is reduced by steady conversation—one on one, in small groups, in big groups.**

The strongest power we have is unity among the majority. Find agreement on something. As you bring more and more people into your conversations, keep your ear open for shared goals—not just shared complaints. Listen, talk, summarize, expand, repeat.

Engage in fear-reducing activities. Where fear is dominant, it's not a good idea to ask people to take risks right away. Asking someone to sign a petition or speak up to a boss may terrify them. Instead, talk through their specific fears and brainstorm how those anticipated disasters could be handled. Ask what information they need to feel safer about taking action, and try to find it. Surface rumors, dissect them, and dispel them.

Invite your co-worker to name others they trust in the workplace, and suggest a group discussion among this cohort. Give an example of how you—or a group—took action and achieved something. Share an article that describes an organizing success among similar workers (*Labor Notes* archives are a great source), and offer to discuss it.

Remember: Don't sell, don't badger, and don't express desperation. All these modes of communication reduce trust and increase fear.

The most likely time your co-workers will begin to act, despite their fear, is when they have generated a plan together as a group. If you come to them insisting on a ready-made strategy, they may dismiss it: "Ha, easy for you to say—you've already got a target on your back."

This doesn't mean you shouldn't come to a meeting prepared with your own ideas, But you should be flexible and make sure that you are genuinely involving others in the discussion, not just getting them to back your idea. (Read more on "Who gets things going" on page 141.)

When people deliberate together, they generate ideas that are grounded in their own experience and that make sense to them. The plans that emerge will be owned by the group, increasing the sense of safety in numbers.

You can start small. Collective action is essential for overcoming fear—but "action" could mean a group of co-workers dividing up a list of names, figuring out who will call whom, agreeing on the goals of those calls, and setting a time to meet again.

The fear of talking to co-workers is the most important fear to overcome—because once *that* action starts, the dynamic of building power has begun, and more action will come.

The fear of talking to co-workers is the most important fear to overcome.

Shame

Shame is a serious obstacle to organizing. People may not tell their co-workers when they get a bad evaluation, get put on a performance improvement plan, or even get fired. It's understandable, but it's isolating, and it undermines the possibility for solidarity.

When we operate under the corrosive influence of shame, we tend to withdraw and become secretive, distrusting, and overly sensitive. Organizing, by contrast, thrives in an atmosphere of openness, self-confidence, trust, and generosity. So organizers should learn how to recognize shame and help people move past it.

Sometimes a bad evaluation is merited. The person is slacking, or always late, or pilfering. But what if it's not, and shame is keeping this individual isolated?

It's not enough to be a cheerleader and say, "No, you don't deserve it, this supervisor was just out to get you." That may make someone feel better, and it's fine as a first step, but it's not going to change the culture in the workplace. The real question is, "Is there anything we can do to help this co-worker to overcome shame, and to start to feel that they're not alone?"

Organizers should learn how to recognize shame and help people move past it.

Ask your co-worker if they're willing to get together with others and talk about the bad evaluation. They may say there's no point (probably out of shame). Show as much patience as you can. It will take time; there is no shortcut. You may need to talk with this person repeatedly. Keep encouraging them—not by guilt-tripping, but by supporting them to feel self-respect.

Ask questions like: "Do you think you're the only person who's ever been retaliated against by this boss?" Probably the answer will be, "Oh no, I think this boss retaliates against people a lot."

Then you might ask, "Do you think these other people might also be feeling bad about it? Did they talk to anyone about it?" "Oh no," the co-worker might respond, "they disappeared and no one heard from them." "Why?" you ask. This kind of conversation will help your co-worker feel less alone.

In one coffee shop, this kind of encouraging conversation led a massive number of workers to begin sharing their evaluations with each other. They posted them on an internal chat group and discovered that the manager was cutting and pasting comments from one to the other, making outrageous assertions, confusing people's job titles and functions, and outright making things up.

The workers found these revelations hilarious, and the discovery brought them together by exposing that the supervisor was not legitimate. Instead of each person fighting alone, they found a sense of collective purpose. It was the first time many of them had had such an experience. It was freeing!

Even when a co-worker has been fired, you may still be able to encourage them to appeal the action, or permit colleagues to fight on their behalf. This is the first step in helping them get past hopelessness and shame—and begin to organize.

We can help people unlearn deeply ingrained patterns of fear, shame, and isolation, which lead to inaction and weak unions. We do it by introducing the possibility of collective power.

Griping and complaining

Complaining isn't the first step to organizing—it's the graveyard of organizing. Just ask any union steward who has listened to a member complain bitterly but refuse to take action.

Complaining isn't the first step to organizing—it's the graveyard of organizing.

There's probably no easier way for co-workers to communicate with each other than by complaining. It's the universal go-to for informal work chat: "Can you believe what he just did?" "What were they thinking?" "I've had it with her!" "If I have to clean up after them one more time…"

Many of us feel that complaining is natural, especially in workplaces that are riddled with problems. If you don't complain, aren't you somehow agreeing with the terrible conditions? Complaining may even seem righteous—and some organizers will tell you it's productive because it brings simmering problems to the surface.

But complaining to "let off steam," if you take no action to change the problem, demonstrates something that's far from organizing: powerlessness. It's like saying, "This thing is wrong, unfair, and hard for me to manage. But now that I've pointed it out, I'm going to go back to living with it, because there's nothing else I can do."

Someone who's complaining is often looking for others to agree. But they may instead polarize co-workers who disagree, creating a toxic, divided atmosphere that undermines the potential for group action.

Complaining can even have the effect of reinforcing the boss's logic. For example, imagine your workplace suffers from understaffing. (This may not take a lot of imagining.) Everyone is under pressure to work harder and faster, to take overtime, to cut corners, to work outside their job duties.

Complaining is the norm. But as soon as someone steps up to suggest that everyone get together to make demands on the boss, the floodgates of "boss logic" will open up. Someone will say, "They don't have the money," or "There's no one out there to hire—they've tried," or "Yeah, but if they hire more staff we'll never get a raise," and on and on. When we're accustomed to having no power, all we're left with are the excuses that the bosses themselves use to maintain the status quo.

The key is to ask thoughtful, respectful questions.

As an organizer, you want to shift how people talk about problems in the workplace. You want your co-workers to get out of the habit of just complaining, and into a new habit that involves analyzing the situation with co-workers, finding common concerns, and making a collective plan of action.

When someone is complaining, engage them with these kinds of questions:

- What's the relevant background (not every gory detail)? What are the facts of the situation (not just your feelings)?
- Who else is affected? Have they been approached?
- Who is creating the problem? Have they been approached?
- What have people tried to fix it? If nothing has been tried, why not?
- What could be done as a first (or next) step? What will the obstacles be?

Each of these questions will open the door to further action steps. For example, if the complainer says he has no idea who else is affected, encourage him to start asking co-workers if they also care about this problem. If he is hesitant, try talking through how those conversations could go. You could even offer to accompany him.

Or if the complainer is stumped about what people could try to fix it, suggest that this question be placed in front of the next union meeting, posed to union officers, or put to members in an open-ended survey.

Key to ending the death-grip of a complaint culture is to ask thoughtful, respectful questions. The organizer's job isn't to "sell" a particular plan of action—it's to confidently assert the idea that a plan of action is possible.

Nobody comes to meetings

In many unions, meetings are notoriously poorly attended. This may be because they're boring—full of routine items like "Old business," "New business," and "Approve the minutes"—or because of practical obstacles that are intrinsic to modern life. Our co-workers have second jobs, opposite schedules, family obligations, and long commutes.

It can help a great deal to offer meetings in different times and places, including at the worksite and online, and to provide food and childcare. It also helps to focus meetings on developing collective plans of action on common concerns. But even when all those criteria are met, most people won't attend most meetings.

How, then, can we organize democratically? Hashing out every decision in a large group meeting might be ideal if we all had several hours a day to meet and talk about our problems—but we don't. So workplace organizers often find strategies to advance group conversation without actually getting everyone in a room at once.

Here's a good technique. The people in the center of the bullseye (see page 142)—those who are acting as organizers—start going out and talking to people, individually or in small groups. They ask questions such as: *What do you think about this issue? Who do you think is affected? What are some goals we might consider? What are some actions we might take?*

With each person you talk to, ask their permission: "I'm going around talking with people. Is it OK if I share with others what we've talked about?" As you go, try to sense where the unity is. Is there something all these people could agree on? You're developing a rough draft of a consensus, based on what you've heard, and testing this assessment with every new conversation.

Say you've had six conversations with individuals, and come to some interim formulation of a problem and its goal. You go back to the first person and say, "Since we talked about this a few days ago, I've had these other conversations with people from six different departments. Here's where I think it's at, based on these conversations. What do you think of that?"

Start going out and talking to people, individually or in small groups.

As soon as you talk to someone who says, "Hmm, I don't think people here would be on board with that plan," then you can start working on it: "OK, what did we miss?" "Do you think if we got together and talked with some of these co-workers they might see what other people are saying and rethink their position? Or do you think this is the bottom line with them?" You may find your original idea does not have sufficient support, and it's back to the drawing board.

BRING THE UNION MEETING TO MEMBERS

Has a co-worker—let's call him Bob—ever asked you, "What happened at the union meeting yesterday?" Did you feel like saying, "You shoulda been there"?

But what does Bob's question tell us about him? That he's more interested than all of the members who have never asked us what happened at the union meeting. Instead of getting mad at Bob for what he doesn't do, we can be glad he's interested—and come up with a small request that he is ready for.

You can make a deal with Bob: If you find him every month and give him a short report from the union meeting, he will agree to pass along the most important points to the co-workers he has lunch with.

To bring the union meeting to even more workers, identify and recruit more volunteers like Bob. You'll be building a communication structure: a member-to-member network.

The most valuable potential volunteers are those who are already trusted by their co-workers. They don't necessarily stand out, so they can go unnoticed by busy activists and union leaders. But

The most valuable potential volunteers are those who are already trusted by their co-workers.

these "most trusteds" usually have similar qualities: They are good workers. They prevent problems for themselves. They listen more than talk, they respect others, and they refrain from gossip, complaining, joining cliques, trashing co-workers, and other drama.

How do you find the most trusteds? Just ask around. Have conversations with groups of workers who work together or go to lunch or break together. Say that you are trying to set up a communication network and you want to approach someone that co-workers trust the most. They don't have to be the most union-involved, just the most trustworthy.

Even if the most trusteds haven't shown much interest in the union up to now, you can ask them to do a small job, as Bob is doing with his co-workers.

When recruiting folks for this job, it's important that you not only tell them what you're asking them to do and why, but also the qualities they have that make them perfect for the job. These folks know that the role they're already playing is important to their co-workers. You can go a long way by communicating that you notice and value them.

—Joe Fahey, retired Teamsters local president

High turnover

Worker churn is everywhere. There are many reasons people come and go—but the worse the job, the higher the churn. And that churn makes workplace organizing more challenging. When your co-workers are coming and going quickly, it's hard to establish the relationships of trust necessary to build power.

Much job churn is the result of big economic forces we don't control. The long-term solution is to make work better, more dignified and decent, through organizing. But in the short run, maybe the best we can do is establish relationships that might make people want to stay.

Greet new co-workers, and be kind, even if you're super-busy. Offer something that might be helpful—like tips on where to find supplies, an introduction to other employees, or a heads-up about a touchy supervisor. Ask what questions they have. Listen to them. This simple act might change their whole attitude about the job.

If your job has a union, offer an informal orientation to the union (or let them know how they can get an official orientation). Give them a copy of the contract, or a link to find it online. Invite everyone to join the union, but don't push them to commit if they're wary. Let them know they can come to you when they're ready.

Establish relationships that might make people want to stay.

Offer new co-workers the opportunity to buddy up with someone more experienced who can be on call to provide the union perspective, suggest how to navigate the workplace, or help them meet other union members.

Bring co-workers into group conversations, in person or online, about things that really matter at the workplace—even if you do it in a casual way. Are there negotiations pending? Is there a problem everyone is talking about, but no plan to address it? Create a culture where your co-workers feel they can learn, ask questions, bring concerns—and be respected. All these things help create a sense of a group—which is a counterweight to the impulse to quit.

Through all these interactions, you're also watching to see what this co-worker might be willing to do in the union. They may not be prepared to make a long-term commitment yet, but they can begin to understand that lending a hand is part of the normal culture. If someone feels respected, wanted, and needed, they're less likely to flee.

In some high-turnover workplaces, organizers have found it necessary to focus on creating a social space, so that workers feel like part of a larger group. In Chicago, the grassroots network Amazonians United has built cohesion among Amazon workers through a group chat, getaways, and get-togethers at restaurants, parks, ice-cream shops, or a neighborhood organization near the warehouse. They also conduct a Union School political education program and hold annual citywide barbecues.

When a co-worker declares they've had it and

they're ready to quit, ask whether they've been anywhere better. The great majority of jobs these days seem to be bad jobs—you're unlikely to find a miraculous good job. Ask, *Is there anything here that's worth preserving and building on? What's worth fighting for?*

Even as we do our best to keep people from quitting, we have to adjust our organizing to reflect the fact of churn. Try to have *two* people team up to do important or recurring tasks so that you're ready when "life happens" and someone disappears. This can also relieve the pressure many of us feel about taking on a commitment when we're not sure how long we'll stick around. Do as much division of labor as possible, so that people aren't wearing seven hats, all of which are left on the ground when they leave.

Every union should have a plan to orient new members. Maybe you have a formal process, or maybe you just have a couple people who watch out for new hires and catch them on a break sometime in the first week to walk them through the essentials. Either way, you should efficiently convey to the newbies what's most important to know about the union. Maybe it's the most common contract violations and how to reach the steward, or maybe it's the story of how we marched on the supervisor and we may have to do it again.

Every union should have a plan to orient new members.

And look on the bright side: If someone has had a positive organizing experience in a workplace, but they job-hop anyway, they can be seeding these good practices wherever they go.

Polarization

This country is sharply divided over partisan politics, immigration, gun control, foreign wars, and questions of race. Your worksite environment may be polarized too.

Even when you're doing something as simple as conducting a bargaining survey, you can run the risk of aggravating these divisions in ways you didn't intend. At the height of the Covid pandemic, for example, a school employees union put out a survey asking members whether they favored a mask mandate, a vaccine mandate, both, or no mandates. Simply asking the question generated fierce pushback and hostility. Some people said, "I'm not even going to respond to this survey because it's clearly partisan. You obviously have bought the whole mask line."

These political divisions are so deeply felt now that the task of bringing people together around common concerns, which sounds pretty straightforward, starts to feel like a minefield. You worry about offending people. It seems safer to do and say nothing.

Workplace organizers should always be thinking about how to bring people together, even when the chasm seems unbridgeable. Ask yourself, "Is there any way to discuss this issue that will help people listen to one another in a non-judgmental way—rather than reinforcing divisions?"

For starters, do not presume there will be agreement. Do not presume that a decision or plan of action will result. Definitely do not demand that everyone choose and declare which side they're on. Hope only that you can introduce and encourage a bit of tolerance that may enable cooperation and action down the road.

Ask open-ended questions. For example, during the height of Covid polarization, you might have asked: "Do you have any health concerns about Covid? Do any family members, friends, or co-workers have concerns? How did they deal with those? Have you heard of any workplaces where the Covid policies made sense to you?" If you can get a non-polarized dialogue going, you can better understand where people are coming from, and perhaps eventually be able to ask those harder, necessary questions.

If distrust is widespread and deeply entrenched, try to find just one or two people from different "camps" who might be open to a conversation aimed at defusing tensions. If this results in some measure of trust, ask these individuals to talk to others in their "camp" to validate the process of dialogue. Once a few people have risked such conversations, a counter-polarizing current may take hold.

> If you can get a non-polarized dialogue going, you can better understand where people are coming from.

Remember that people need a strong motivation to engage in these depolarizing conversations. The motivation can't be to win a debate, expose the other side as villainous, or justify a sense of self-righteousness. The motivation that worksite organizers should consistently encourage is the imperative of unity—the thing that is essential to changing the balance of power between workers and the boss. If this is a shared goal, steadily bring co-workers back to it. Polarizing differences may begin to lose their destructive grip.

A good method is the one used by a caucus in the Massachusetts Teachers Association to talk about the crisis in Gaza (see pages 198–9). Despite the fact that members of this caucus share a lot of political beliefs, the conflict on this issue threatened to create distrust and divisions. Their approach could be sturdy enough to help other groups navigate wrenching divisions over a wide variety of different issues.

LISTEN FIRST

Educators for a Democratic Union, a caucus in the Massachusetts Teachers Association, decided in 2023 that members needed to talk about the crisis in Gaza. Feelings were running very high, and some unions around the country were fracturing. EDU wanted to create a platform for discussion first, before any formal union action. We invited caucus members to an emergency meeting to discuss the occupation and war.

The meeting was framed as an opportunity to listen to each other, not a space for decision-making or debate. Members were asked to reflect on their experiences and perspectives at this moment and each was given two minutes to speak. We were clear that this was a gathering of unionists and that the beauty and difficulty of union work is that we come together not because we share a point of view, but because we are workers.

People spoke of terrible grief and the struggle to find hope. They spoke of family members who it was suddenly difficult to speak to, or family members they now feared for. Some focused on how we build unity in the moment, others on defending members being doxxed for speaking out in support of Palestine. Some talked about protests they had attended or organized.

After we listened, we went into breakouts based on some of the ideas that had come up: calling for a ceasefire; defending those being silenced; speaking to co-workers; direct actions; and talking about this in our classrooms. Groups then reported on ideas and some made plans for next steps.

While differences remained, we were able to hear each other and moved toward some consensus. One shared understanding was that we needed to think of whatever we did in the context of organizing—of talking to people and listening to them.

—Barbara Madeloni, Labor Notes staff organizer and EDU member

Accused of bullying

The more confidently workers start organizing to improve things, the more aggressively the boss may shut you down. They may accuse the active unionist of being a troublemaker, which should be considered a badge of honor. They've noticed the ground shifting under their feet.

But what if the shop floor organizer is accused of being a bully? The boss will claim to be defending other workers—always unnamed—from unwanted attention or haranguing. Sometimes it's true that a co-worker may not want to be bothered. But mostly this is just a tactic to chill your organizing. Don't get stuck in fear or self-doubt. If you know you're not a bully, stand up to the accusation. Demand proof of the charge, and defend your right to organize on the shop floor.

A young food service worker was fed up with the inadequate ventilation and mercilessly hot temperatures in the kitchen and dishwashing room. As a good organizer, he talked with co-workers to get their opinions and start formulating an action plan. Quick as a wink, he got a discipline letter for bullying. For a minute he panicked, but then self-respect kicked in. With support from a strong steward and an emerging atmosphere of solidarity among union members, he fought back. At

Bullying is the misuse of power by someone who has it, against someone who doesn't.

the grievance hearing he got the manager to admit that he had every right to talk about workplace issues during work hours. The "charges" of bullying from co-workers were unprovable and evaporated.

Remember that bullying is the misuse of power by someone who has it, against someone who doesn't. When you talk with co-workers about workplace problems, that could be uncomfortable. Maybe they are not affected and would prefer to be left alone; maybe they are scared of retaliation; maybe they are confused by your interest. But none of this is bullying. Shrug it off and keep going.

Too few people doing too much work

It's a common situation: There's too much union work to do, and not enough people doing it. And the ill effects are serious.

Carrying too much work puts a lot of pressure on you, and you're liable to burn out. You may find yourself overwhelmed with tasks, unable to prioritize, and dissatisfied with the results. And you may be making poor decisions, because you're too busy to solicit and include ideas from others. As a result, you're squandering the most essential thing: the intelligence, creativity, and energy that your fellow members could bring.

Unfortunately, the most common "solutions" rarely work:

- Grabbing whoever is nearest at hand and begging them to take over some job.
- Scolding members: "*Don't blame the union if stuff isn't getting done. If more members don't step up and get involved, what do you expect?*"
- Posting general appeals in the union newsletter: "*Get involved! Join a committee! Run for office!*"
- Piling one more task onto someone who doesn't know how to say no.

One approach is to change how you're asking individuals to join you. It's possible that some of your co-workers are waiting to be invited into meaningful dialogue and work—but they may not know it until you invite them. Make a list of people you'd like to see step up, and try this:

- **Offer an invitation, not an "assignment."** Let's not treat fellow union members the way the boss treats us. Invite your co-workers to think together about what the union is doing or could be doing.
- **Follow their lead.** The best bet is to just ask them what they think is important. Where do they think the union has been falling down? What is it doing well? Is there anything they're curious about? Ask what they're good at, what they enjoy doing, what they're keen to learn. Maybe there's something intriguing but intimidating that they might try if they could set conditions on it. Keep asking questions till you find a spark.
- **Create tasks based on what they want to do.** You probably feel there's a long list of things that must be done, but give it a fresh look. Maybe there are different ways to accomplish a goal, or new ideas that come from conversation with the prospective activist. A good leader fashions a plan that reflects members' ideas and helps them blossom.

- **Bring dignity and care to the task.** Dignify whatever contribution a member can make, even if it seems small to you. Help them think through a task step by step, and honor each effort.
- **Offer a work buddy.** When someone is coming into union work for the first time, they'll benefit from having someone they can go to for questions and encouragement.
- **Relinquish control.** Since you've been doing so much, you may have gotten used to the feeling of being "in charge" of union stuff. When other members step up, step back and make space for them.

Beyond recruiting individuals, can you create welcoming opportunities for group participation?

A union in Virginia had suffered under inept leadership for many years, until nearly all the work was being done by one person—the president—who thought this arrangement was fine.

A small group of disgruntled members set out to transform the union. They wanted to bring other members in, but there was nothing to bring them to—no membership meetings, no committees, no campaigns, not even a newsletter or bulletin board. So, without permission from the president, they organized a "Workers Assembly" where anyone could come share their experiences and listen. They made clear that this wasn't a "union meeting" and there wouldn't be any "official" business.

The meeting was lively and respectful, and it proved to be a magnet. Workers who had never stepped into any union space before showed up to this and subsequent assemblies. As issues surfaced in the discussions, some people got curious about how they could start taking action to address them. The core group grew. Some newly activated members started a newsletter, others got involved in preparing for collective bargaining, and others began helping co-workers solve problems on the job. Eventually a caucus took shape and won leadership of the union.

What about when a specific role has to be filled? A union representing a high-turnover workplace faced this problem. Union roles were often vacant, so vital union work piled up on the remaining officers and stewards. And then, with negotiations looming, a co-president abruptly had to step down for personal reasons.

The remaining co-president needed to find a replacement, quick. But everyone active in the union was already overwhelmed. What could she do?

At an executive board meeting, she asked everyone to write down the qualities and skills they thought would be ideal in the next co-president. They discussed their ideas and agreed on a list. Then she handed out a spreadsheet showing every member who had engaged with the union in some way over the last couple of years—they'd been a steward, volunteered for a committee, run for office, joined a bargaining or contract action team, attended a rally or meeting, or baked cookies.

She asked the board members to scrutinize the list of needed skills and qualities, and then the spreadsheet. Anyone who met a plausible number of criteria should be written down as a possible candidate. She encouraged them not to preemptively exclude anyone ("I know she's way too busy") and urged them to also consider themselves.

The exercise showed a pretty wide circle of people who could fill the role, with half a dozen leading candidates, including some current board members. None declined to be considered. Probably some were hesitant about the new responsibility, but they also felt honored enough to rise to the occasion. People volunteered to reach out to the other candidates.

By this time the desperation had drained away, replaced by a sense of confidence. The collective process had a strength and credibility that was very different than if the co-president had tried to recruit someone on her own.

In follow-up conversations, one especially well-suited candidate emerged. But to take the role, she would have to step down from chairing an important union committee. No problem: Another of the candidates would be perfect for that committee! He agreed to do it, but he would have to step away as department steward—so he recruited another co-worker for that job. A virtuous cycle rolled out in front of everyone's eyes.

A leader gets fired

Firing a workplace leader is a classic union-busting tactic. The employer hopes to create a chilling effect, discouraging anyone else from sticking their necks out. Often it works.

When someone who has been outspoken gets fired, other workers will be watching closely to see what happens next. They will draw a lesson about whether the union has power—can it protect this person?—and whether courageous action is worthwhile.

The union should pursue every formal remedy available, like filing grievances and unfair labor practice charges. But those processes will likely take months or years, and you can't guarantee the results. It can also reinforce people's sense of powerlessness in the workplace, if it seems like the union's only answer is waiting for a distant authority to step in.

So from an organizing perspective, while you take those steps, it's important that you and your co-workers also continue finding ways to show that your bonds of solidarity are only getting stronger and are a force of defense.

A good example is the union campaign at a transit agency in Alexandria, Virginia. Shortly after bus drivers won their unionization drive 97 to 13, the employer fired a key leader.

Organizers filed unfair labor practice charges. At the same time, to shore up workers' confidence, they redoubled their efforts to involve as many people as possible in visible collective actions. The bargaining team set out to talk with every driver about their priorities for the first contract, including people who had voted no. Drivers joined public actions like leafleting riders and packing a city council meeting.

It was important that the firing of the popular leader not go unanswered. The union found her another job at a unionized facility and kept inviting her to meetings—making clear that no one was giving up on her. A large majority of the drivers signed a petition demanding her reinstatement, and this demand became a central plank in the contract campaign.

To exhaust all avenues, the union also contested the termination through the company's phony grievance procedure, which required her to pay $100 for her case to be heard. Members used the opportunity to show that they had her back—100 drivers each donated $1.

When the drivers won their first contract, her reinstatement was part of the deal. The cherry on top: The agency fired the manager who had fired her.

Burnout and discouragement

In the early months of the Covid pandemic, everyone was burned out. Everyone was discouraged. Workers wondered who was making the Covid decisions at their workplace, and why they were changing every day. Some workers saw their workloads double. Some experienced new extremes of micromanagement. And everyone was worried about when they, their families, their co-workers, or their customers or patients or students were going to get sick.

The pull to give up, to withdraw, to hunker down and "just survive" was almost irresistible—perhaps even for a committed activist like you, the reader of this book.

But in spite of everything, some people managed to connect with one another at work, even if just through images on a screen. Some of us who were hunkering down came to know that others were in the same situation. And we remembered that the fight we were already committed to—for decent, dignified work and the power needed to win it—was always going to be a long and hard haul.

Here are some of the lessons learned. These apply any time when burnout and discouragement threaten to swamp you and your co-workers.

Count on your values. Remind yourself what you believe and how you want to act on your beliefs. Those have not changed just because the employer has found a new way to slap us around. When the boss implements an awful new policy, you have a choice: shoulder it without question, complain bitterly, or think critically about a response.

If your values include self-respect and respect for your co-workers, then the first two options make no sense. Accepting abuse is incompatible with your values. Just complaining is an advertisement of powerlessness. Why not start with the intention to resist?

Broadcast determination. Even if you can barely scrape yourself off the ground, don't broadcast despair to co-workers. The tendency toward hopeless dismay is very contagious, but so is determination not to give up. Commiseration and complaining are a waste of time. But engaging your co-workers about productive ways to resist is gold.

Consider how often you've found yourself thinking that most of your co-workers are apathetic or frightened or just go along to get along. These are the attitudes that people take on when they have given in to helplessness.

You steadily assert confidence that things can change through collective action.

Your commitment to resisting oppression should help you reach past your co-workers' defenses. You steadily assert confidence that things can change through collective action. No need for false optimism or cheerleading; just be doggedly committed to your own dignity—and theirs.

Set a real goal. Some goal is better than no goal. It doesn't help to be overly ambitious ("We need to get rid of this guy," or "Let's all walk out right now," or

"I'm refusing to follow that policy no matter what"). Start with the simple conviction that *something* can be done, that some action can be taken together with co-workers.

Setting any goal that can be achieved is a far better use of your energy than setting a wildly unrealistic goal too soon. Is a realistic goal just to talk with colleagues and encourage them? Then choose that.

Start with the simple conviction that something can be done.

Maybe your next goal is to get together with co-workers to ask the boss probing questions about the new policy. In lots of workplaces this itself will be seen as insurrection, and people will need coaching and encouragement to take such a step.

It's the attitude of collective noncompliance that matters: noncompliance with the fear that pervades the worksite, with the employer's right to be unilateral and coercive, and with the "normal" subordinate behavior that's expected of workers. Practicing noncompliance in small but purposeful ways builds the muscle of collective power and pushes against helplessness.

Extend grace to your co-workers. Since our only path to power at work is through collective action, the need to connect with co-workers is beyond debate. But maybe your workplace is rife with gossip, cliques, racist hostility, competitive friction, or distrust. Or maybe there's so much turnover that you barely know your colleagues.

None of this is a reason not to strive to get along with the people you work with. No one can get along with *everyone* they work with. But in any workplace you can set a reasonable goal of positive connection with potential allies.

When a co-worker snaps at you, don't snap back. If you admire the way a colleague has conducted herself, tell her. If someone in your workplace is driving himself too hard, help him regain perspective and slow down. If someone is in despair, show her your trust.

Bad union leadership

If you're bursting with organizing ideas and union leaders shut you down, often it's because your ideas make no sense to them.

People in union office tend to follow the rules of the system they inherit. Maybe they're clinging to familiar old patterns because they're overwhelmed, underprepared, or beset by pressures from different constituencies. Maybe they think the union's power is limited to filing grievances, and they have little experience with doing things differently.

Don't assume bad faith. The first step might be to talk directly with the union leaders. It's important that this not be an emotional confrontation. Be calm, curious, and respectful. Be prepared with concrete examples of what you and others have experienced, and with suggestions for how things could be improved. For example, you could suggest that the union should:

- Schedule meetings more regularly, at times and places most accessible to members.
- Seek input from members for the meeting agendas.
- Use meetings not only for officer reports, but also to promote discussion.
- Open up processes previously conducted "confidentially," such as bargaining, grievance representation, labor-management meetings, and so on.

Your union leaders may turn out to welcome your ideas and your participation after all.

On the other hand, they may reject your suggestions. They may feel you are assaulting their integrity or competence, or trying to "steal" their power. They might react defensively and double down on excluding you. In the worst cases, union leaders even collude with management to bear down on a "troublemaker."

Sadly, plenty of union leaders believe that unions should be top-down, with a small group controlling all the important information, decisions, and actions. How many times have you heard that grievances can't be discussed with the membership because of "confidentiality"? How often are months of contract negotiations reduced to a terse report that "progress is being made on Article 17, Section 5"?

This withholding of information isn't required by law, it's just widespread in union culture and practice. The effect is to keep members uninformed and distant from decision-making.

These kinds of leaders likely have many explanations about why member engagement won't work: *Members don't come to meetings. They don't read their email. They're complacent. They expect me to do everything. They're too scared. They only care about their own problems.*

Rather than take responsibility to educate, consult, and engage members, these leaders dismiss them.

The underlying dynamic is disrespect. When leaders don't trust the members, they can disregard them. Members feel disdained and excluded, and therefore withdraw. Such a hollowed-out union is weak. It doesn't pose much of a threat to the boss.

If your leaders aren't the ones you hoped for, it may be up to you to change the culture and shape the future of your union. As in any union situation, don't act alone. Talk to co-workers. Your purpose isn't to convince anyone, but simply to ask questions. For example:

- How do you think we're doing as a union?
- Are you able to get information and questions answered?
- Have you been active in the union, or tried to get active? What was that like?
- Are there things you'd like to see the union doing?

You could start by finding a workplace issue that co-workers care about, bringing them together to talk about it, and developing a plan for action. You may want to keep your union leaders informed, but don't ask for their permission.

If there's inadequate information flowing in the union, start an informal channel to share and solicit ideas—but don't let it become a gripe-fest. Reach out to other groups that should be allies and open up conversations about common concerns.

Don't ask for permission.

Once you initiate these conversations, you may be targeted. If this happens to you, stay steady, organize, and persevere. Be strategic rather than angry. Don't attack the leader or spread hostility. Instead, focus on building a base and taking action. Find a cluster of other union members who are ready to do something.

Consider a caucus. In the end, if you find that you can't move your local in a more democratic, inclusive, and activist direction, you might consider starting a rank-and-file caucus to open up the question of what kind of union the members really prefer.

Rank-and-file caucuses have a long and proud tradition in U.S. unions. A caucus is simply a group of members who are dedicated to improving their union. Often the motivation for creating a caucus is a lack of transparency in the union, leaders' unwillingness to fight, or too much coziness with the boss. A caucus may start by organizing around issues, and end up challenging the current leaders in union elections.

If you do decide to go down the caucus path, prepare yourself for a lot of heartbreak along the way. It's likely the incumbent leaders will accuse you of being divisive or even anti-union. They will likely question your motives and make bogus accusations about your methods.

But democratizing our unions is essential to rebuilding our power. And it's worth every hard, uncomfortable, and heartbreaking moment.

WHEN YOUR EMPLOYER, A UNION, BREAKS YOUR HEART

What if, as a union staffer, you are not permitted to support bottom-up decision-making?

Maybe the union you work for has a top-down culture, reinforced through hierarchical staff management, where organizers are just expected to implement plans devised above. You're required to meet strict metrics—how many one-on-one conversations to have, what to say, quotas of pledge cards to collect, and so on. But you have no space to bring workers together to develop their own plans. You might even be reprimanded or face serious discipline for not staying "on program."

There are two separate questions here. One is whether union staff, like all other workers, deserve a union to bargain their own wages, hours, and working conditions. They do! Union staffers can follow the advice in this book: Bring co-workers together, discuss shared concerns, set goals, and plan actions to have a collective say.

> How can you best support members in democratically transforming the union?

But the focus of this book is how democratizing can make our unions more powerful. If you're a union staffer, the main question is how you can best support the members in democratically transforming the union. This might mean a certain kind of organizing training, labor education, or putting members in touch with others who have transformed their unions.

Encourage their initiative. Recognize that this is *their* task, not your task. As an employee of the union, you have resources to offer and support to give, but the decision about what kind of union to build is in the members' hands.

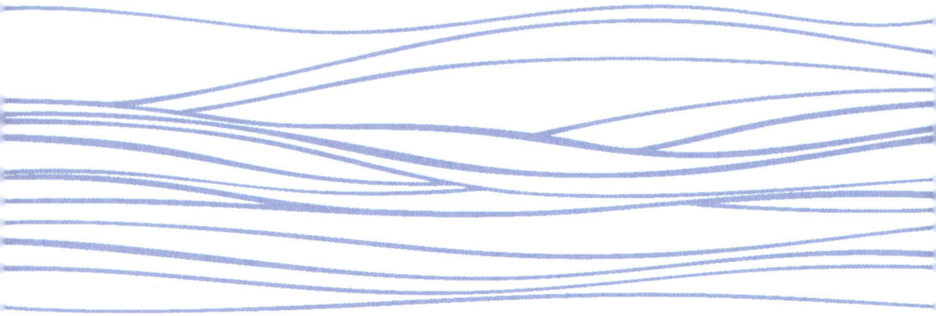

PART IV: THINK AGAIN...

We pick up organizing methods from various sources. We draw lessons from our own experiences, but often also from union training workshops, advice from fellow organizers, and books like this one. Maybe you're faithfully following the advice you've gotten, but the results aren't what you expected. Now what?

There's a lot of organizing advice out there, but it's not all compatible with the values and long-haul approach described in this book. Techniques meant for top-down, short-term mobilizing may actually get in your way if your goal is to develop trusting relationships and the collective confidence it takes to shift the balance of power in your workplace long-term.

If you're trying to organize "by the book" but it's not working so well, this section may help you identify why. Embracing democratic principles might require breaking some ingrained habits. Or you might heave a sigh of relief when you get permission to let go of some unpleasant practices you had been told were necessary!

Selling the union

Do you sometimes feel like an infomercial for the union, talking up its benefits and downplaying its flaws? It's understandable—you want as many co-workers as possible to come together and build something powerful. But people hate the hard sell. Don't you get suspicious when someone is trying too hard to convince you of something?

It's especially challenging if in truth your union *hasn't* been doing a great job, and your co-workers just don't buy your claims about its potential.

You've wandered especially far afield if you find yourself trying to sell people on products the union provides that have nothing to do with organizing, such as life insurance, discount travel plans, buying club cards, or raffles. A handful of unions even offer cash bonuses for members who recruit other members, as though the union were a pyramid scheme. That's not what building collective power looks like.

Organizing isn't based on convincing people, but on engaging them. Try approaching each co-worker with real curiosity: What are they spending their time on? What do they care about? What makes them "not care" about the union? Who do they respect among their colleagues, and why? What are they proud of about their own work?

Organizing isn't based on convincing people, but on engaging them.

Then ponder with them how the union could become a place where they feel welcome, useful, and connected to others. What is something you could do to help this person move toward the union?

There's no need to argue or defend anything; that sets you up on opposite sides with your co-workers. Assume they want things to improve, but they don't see how they can. It's fine to share your enthusiasm and why you care about the union—but do it without pressure. Build trust by listening.

Agitation

You may have been told that, once you find a workplace issue your co-worker cares about, you've got to whip them into anger over it, with agitational questions like "Is that OK with you?" and "How long are you willing to let that go on?" These pointed questions are meant to inflame a righteous indignation strong enough to overcome their fear and get them to commit to taking action.

But if their commitment to action is based on momentary emotion, will it hold firm after that emotion passes? And if your co-worker is left feeling that you pressured and manipulated them into a commitment they're not so sure about once they have sobered up, how are they going to feel about you? What if you keep doing that to them over and over, because it's your go-to organizing method?

If you want to build a relationship of trust and respect with your co-workers, sometimes you'll be better served by calming down the emotion in your organizing conversations, not whipping it up. Read more about "getting off the roller coaster" on page 88.

The scripted "ask"

You're having a conversation with a co-worker, but inside you're feeling icy dread. You're talking through a script that ends with asking them to do a specific thing: sign a union card, wear a button, come to a meeting, vote for a strike. And sure enough, when you ask, a wall comes down. The co-worker looks away, makes an excuse, and pins you as someone who is after something. You're disappointed, confused about why it didn't work, and afraid you're not going to meet your goal.

Many of us feel nervous or awkward about asking a co-worker to do something. Sometimes we just need to push ourselves to do it. But if you're being pressured to follow the script and get to a particular "ask" without finding out who this person is and moving at their pace, that's a problem. A co-worker you don't yet have much of a relationship with may be turned off that you're pressuring them to take an action that has already been decided on by others.

Replace the "ask" (to take some predetermined action) with an invitation.

What can you do instead? Replace the "ask" (to take some predetermined action) with an invitation: "Hey, some of us are getting together to talk about this. You want to join us?" "Can we figure out how you can be part of the solution to this problem that you're posing?"

People are happy to be asked to do something they want to do, that they're good at, that they're confident about. People like to be asked to do things when it reflects your respect for them: "*You're asking me to do this because you're confident in my ability. You know I like this task, or that I'm good at it.*" Think how different that is from simply complying with what the organizer wants them to do.

A young worker in a chemical factory in Massachusetts was trying to interest his co-workers in a union. After many frustrating weeks of trying to approach people with an ask—to come to a meeting with a union organizer—he was about to give up. But then he opened his eyes to other possibilities and changed his approach: "What I'm really trying to do is build real relationships," he said. "I decided to see what happened if I gave up the ask."

With this new approach, in a matter of just two or three weeks, he met his goal to connect with co-workers in a dozen departments where he had not previously had any contact. He found that it was so much easier to make contact when that was the only goal. What had been holding him back from contacting these people before? "I didn't know what the ask was. And what do they owe me? They're going to feel bad if they don't do what I ask. They might avoid me."

Instead, his co-workers started to approach him with questions, concerns, and ideas about workplace problems. It emerged that the boss was providing very different retirement packages to different employees. Pretty soon a group came together to document the problem, propose a fix, and bring it to the boss.

Any hard "ask" should stem from inclusive discussion and collective decisions.

Of course organizers are asking people to do things all the time—our organizing is about action, not just talk. And there are times when making a specific ask, even pushing hard, makes sense—asking people to commit to a strike, for instance, or to vote yes in a union election. But such urgency should be grounded in strong relationships and discussions that have built trust over time, helping people overcome fear. Any hard "ask" should stem from inclusive discussion and collective decisions. People should be coming up to you to say, "Is that petition what I think it is? Give me that, I want to sign it."

Over-promising

Let's say that cynicism surrounds you on all sides. Over and over, your union has fallen short of members' expectations.

You might be tempted to promise your co-worker that if she gets involved, the results will be far better. But be careful!

How can you, or anyone, know what the outcome of a fight will be? It depends not only on how many people join the effort, but also on other factors you can't foresee or control. If you make promises that aren't achieved, you may fuel disappointment and even more cynicism.

If you make promises that aren't achieved, you may fuel disappointment.

Plus, if you're the one making promises, the implication is that you're the one who can deliver. But an organizer is a connector, not a "fixer." Your job is to bring people together and ask, "What do we think we, as a group, can do?"

There is one promise you *can* make: If more and more co-workers begin to really talk together, and get past complaining to take some group action together (no matter how small), then *something* will change. At minimum, people will feel less alone and less afraid. They will start to feel more respect for each other, and develop a more shared sense of purpose. And from this, power can grow.

Cheerleading

Have you been taught to hype up every fight as extremely high-stakes, and every small gain as historic, in an effort to propel campaigns forward with the sheer force of your enthusiasm?

After every campaign, do you find a way to declare a union victory, fearing that your co-workers would lose faith if you had an honest discussion of a setback or a mixed bag? Show them more respect—they can handle complexity.

Your organizing will be stronger if it relies less on propaganda and allows for more honest discussion among members. See chapter 8 for ways to reflect on a campaign that can move you forward positively without sugarcoating anything.

Constant urgency

Organizing drives and other union campaigns are often frantic. Frequently we're facing some hard deadline, like a contract expiration date. On top of that, many of us have been trained that setting intermediate deadlines helps us get things done—which is true.

But too much urgency can deter our efforts to build a sustainable, democratic union culture. Sometimes we need to slow down.

Be realistic about how long it will take to build relationships, work through differences, calm fears, and plan for actions. Reflect on what the source of urgency is, and whether you can alter it. We don't control a lot of things, but we can try to control our own organizing timelines.

A rank-and-file nurse was trying to collect union authorization cards on a short deadline, hoping to lessen the boss's time to run a union-busting campaign. After some initial success, she noticed that support was starting to fall off. Her co-workers were avoiding her. They had just shut down.

> Too much urgency can deter our efforts to build a sustainable, democratic union culture.

She was working with a union staffer who had set the deadlines and card-collection quotas. The nurse's instinct was to slow down, get to know what her co-workers were thinking, answer their questions, and work through their fears. But the staff organizer's response was: "No, you just need to push people forward. It may be hard, but you need to keep momentum. I've been through this many times before. If you slow down now, people will lose confidence and they'll want to give up. The main thing is to get the cards signed, call an election, and get an election. You can keep building those relationships afterwards."

This is pretty standard advice for a union campaign, but is it the best approach? The employer's union-busting campaign does take a serious toll, but so does a lack of confidence and unity. Both can cause us to lose elections. Often it takes years and several tries for a group of workers to win a union.

Most workers aren't familiar with unions. Presumably they do want to earn a better wage or improve working conditions, but whether a union can really achieve that is a big unknown. And most people are (quite reasonably) afraid of retaliation from their boss. They're accustomed to an attitude of compliance and fear in the workplace.

The antidote to this deeply ingrained fear is building solid relationships based on experiences: "*I know who you are. You did what you said you were going to do, and the results were what we expected. We survived it, we talked about it afterwards, and we kept working together.*" This is how people come to believe in their collective power and establish trust.

Can you just get the union cards signed first (or the picket commitments, etc.) and then build relationships of trust later? This isn't going to be helpful in the long run.

People come to the party they're invited to. You're not just trying to get co-workers to "do something" but rather to join you in building a durable, democratic organization.

When you first approach co-workers, you start to create the culture of the union you're trying to build. It's not impossible to rebuild a culture—but if you're starting from scratch, it's a good idea to build the kind of union that you'd actually like to have. And those reasons for urgency won't be going away.

So consider slowing down. This takes confidence in yourself. Don't get distracted or disappointed by a slow pace or defeats along the way. Every step is a learning experience.

From the beginning, build the kind of union you'd actually like to have.

Waiting for the perfect moment

Sometimes energy bubbles up spontaneously. The boss has done something so intolerable that people come together and want to take action. Somehow people find each other and, seemingly without any real planning, take concerted action.

Plenty of organizers yearn for these moments and regard them as golden organizing opportunities—the sparks that can be fanned into wildfire.

Don't be in such a hurry that you forget democracy or strategy.

But the truth is, this sequence of events is very rare. We can't pin our organizing plans on it. How many times have we seen a "hot issue" explode and then fizzle? And even when a spontaneous uprising does happen, it may not be such a great opportunity for ongoing organizing. Because if it's spontaneous, we don't know how it started, or how to keep it going.

We can't depend on something happening that is so terrible, it will push people to act. That's not how most workplaces are, most of the time. If your organizing relies on people being motivated by a crisis, then you may have to wait a long time. There's always plenty of bad stuff happening, but it's constant and low-level, so people accommodate themselves to it. They think, "This is just what I have to bear." So don't wait—get started.

You should still take advantage of unexpected organizing opportunities, but watch out for the pitfalls of spontaneous action: Don't be in such a hurry that you forget democracy or strategy. Have you taken time to consult others? Have you thought through the possible consequences?

What if the boss gets really fierce and fires people? Will this deflate everyone—and leave you with no Plan B? Or the boss says, "OK, OK, I'll do what you want," the air deflates… and then the boss doesn't do what you wanted, and you're all demobilized.

Even when you're feeling the heat of the moment, take the time to consider: Do you have enough people? What action should you take? If you don't think all this through, then you're squandering some power and a chance to increase democratic participation.

Confidentiality

Secrecy should not be the default in union work.

Maybe you're trying to organize a union, and everyone is afraid of boss retaliation. So you're keeping things very quiet—but wondering how you can actually reach everyone this way.

Or maybe you're in a union where the officers are doing a poor job. You're trying to start a rank-and-file caucus, but members are scared of retribution from their own officers. So you're doing it pretty secretly, and the group isn't growing beyond a handful of activists.

Or perhaps you're a steward and you've started to see a pattern in the grievances. You'd like to start talking to members about how they can come together as a group to deal with the wider underlying problem. But you've been warned that all grievances are strictly confidential, so you hold back.

Confidentiality isn't a rule; it's just part of a culture. And sometimes we should rethink it.

There are times when confidentiality is appropriate. If a member is in the middle of a very sensitive grievance and adamantly insists on holding things in confidence, no problem. Early in a union organizing drive, it may also be smart to keep things on the down-low, so you don't trigger the boss's anti-union campaign before you have built the strength to withstand it.

But secrecy should not be the default in union work.

Whenever information is withheld, it means there are some people in the know, and many who aren't. Secrecy sets up a hierarchy that carries the message: *The rest of you aren't as important, and your ideas don't matter. Let us make the decisions and tell you the outcome—or not.*

When information isn't flowing freely, it opens up space for gossip, speculation, rumors, paranoia, and confusion. This is fertile soil for distrust to grow—among members or between members and officers. And even worse, it can lead workers to disengage.

Secrecy among co-workers breeds weakness. The employer thrives as the definitive source of information, and will readily use that power to their own advantage—withholding information, giving it out differentially, or spreading disinformation. When building a democratic union, our goal is the opposite—to spread power widely, not hoard it.

When stewards in one union started tracking all their grievances in a shared spreadsheet, they started finding actionable patterns. Many supervisors were applying similar unfair hiring practices. The stewards realized the problem was emanating from H.R. policies, and that their most effective strategy would be to advance one big dispute that could create change across the board, rather than fighting one case after another with individual supervisors who didn't have the power to fix the problem.

Waiting for permission to act

Many workers have grown accustomed to problems going unsolved. They don't expect the supervisor, H.R., or anyone to really listen and fix things. But they *should* expect that, when they're going to the union with a problem, there will be a plan of action.

Unfortunately, too often they're told to wait for the grievance procedure and not do anything else. And then the grievance procedure takes forever to resolve. What do you do while you're waiting?

There's another way to go. Any group of workers can meet, talk about the problem, come up with a plan, and carry it out. That's the real spirit of unionism. Waiting for someone else to give you permission tends to reinforce a feeling of powerlessness. Taking any action, no matter how small—as long as it's done by a group—is empowering. Don't wait!

It's not always as simple as saying "go." Waiting and hoping that someone else will fix things can become a deeply ingrained habit. Your fellow union members may feel hesitant to act because they're loyal to officers or staff, even if those people haven't proven very effective. They may feel it's impolite or against union rules to take action without a stamp of approval. Even calling a meeting yourselves may seem transgressive and a little scary.

Any group of workers can meet, talk about the problem, come up with a plan, and carry it out.

Be patient and reassuring. Show people that waiting isn't the only option. Stimulate discussion about what else can be done from the bottom up.

You may encounter friction from officers or staff who feel that it's their job to run the union. They may frown on independent actions, try to squash them, or try to take over. They might move like molasses when members are asking for something, but when members start acting, they move like lightning to take back control. Help your colleagues prepare for this and hold steady with their plans, even against the objections of officers or staff.

Bargaining surveys

The typical bargaining survey has a problem: It's a one-way communication.

Plenty of unions make no effort to ask members about their priorities before negotiations, so circulating a survey is certainly a positive step. However, the typical bargaining survey has a problem: It's a one-way communication.

The survey asks about topics that the union leadership has probably already decided are important. It may ask about wages, for instance, but not get into issues of dignity and respect on the job, which are often at the top of everyone's list.

A reform caucus in a union put out a survey after management made a schedule change. The survey asked, "How did this change affect you? Did it make things worse or better? What are your feelings about it?" Most of the responses said: "The worst thing is that nobody was asked for input. It's characteristic of the disrespect that we've gotten used to seeing."

Most bargaining surveys don't ask questions like that. So the leaders may miss some of the most important things going on for their members.

Another shortcoming of the typical bargaining survey is that it's often the last time in the bargaining process that the union leadership communicates with members about what they want. When the needs that members expressed aren't addressed, they have good reason to feel sour: "*Well, you asked me, but you didn't give it to me. So obviously you don't respect me, or didn't fight, or weren't listening.*"

These problems can be addressed if you take a different approach, starting with the survey. Ask open-ended questions: "What are your biggest problems in the workplace? And as you look around, what are the biggest problems you see your co-workers facing?"

Another improvement is to conduct the survey in person, not in writing. Reaching out to people face to face generates a valuable back-and-forth between the surveyor and the surveyed. And it indicates greater respect, because it takes more time.

Even if you're not able to conduct the initial survey in person, you can summarize the responses to a written survey and bring co-workers together to talk about them: "*Here's what we heard. Here's the number of people who identified x as an issue.*"

If people are nearly unanimous about a certain issue, have a discussion about how to proceed on it. And where there is division, consider together: How can we maximize our strength, despite our different priorities?

Which bargaining items are most important? What can we trade, and what should we hold out on? How can we make sure the largest number of members come out much better off in this contract?

All this discussion, which usually happens only within the bargaining team, can be brought to a number of meetings so that as many people

If you can't do the survey face to face, gather to discuss the results.

as possible get the chance to participate. The results can be summarized into a general platform, and members can vote on whether to ratify it.

All this is time- and labor-intensive. But it engages members seriously in the contract campaign, sets the stage for the bargaining team to keep consulting with members during negotiations, and develops a sense of unified purpose.

Bargaining behind closed doors

In some unions, ratification of a collective bargaining agreement can leave members feeling alienated and angry. They had little or no communication from the bargaining team during negotiations. Maybe they didn't even know what the union was proposing.

One way to build a powerful, participatory, energized union is by opening up bargaining. If you're in union leadership, below are some practices you could implement. If you're a rank-and-file caucus, you can push for them.

> Open bargaining can start no matter where you are in the bargaining cycle.

You don't have to wait until negotiations begin. Open bargaining can start no matter where you are in the bargaining cycle. At every phase, there's a way to educate members and empower them to lead.

Contract education sessions. These can be short and specific: 10-minute shop floor meetings to learn about specific terms and conditions in your current contract. For example, one meeting could focus on the provisions for paid time off.

These can be offered regularly, every week or month, in person or online. They might focus on the contract language that's most relevant to the problems members are having. It's a chance to teach, but also to ask: What could be clarified or strengthened? What's missing? Invite people to brainstorm new language.

Keep notes. Ask if they want to help draft new proposals for the next contract.

Discuss bargaining priorities. Think beyond a one-time bargaining survey (see page 240). Priorities should be worked out through discussion among the members who will live under the contract. Schedule regular consultation chats with groups of members.

Ask them to grapple with conflicting priorities. As people listen to each other, shared priorities can come to the fore and minimize the feeling that members are competing with one another for a piece of the pie.

Contract topic committees. In many unions, the members are entirely left out of drafting and revising proposals. Think how that squanders members' potential wisdom, passion, and experience—not to mention volunteer labor! Instead, the union should offer support—meeting space, background material, facilitation—for numerous committees to form and meet regularly.

It's never too soon to form a committee of rank and filers who track a certain issue—for instance, wage structure, health insurance, schedules, evaluation and discipline, paid leave time, or health and safety—and think about what members need in that area.

It's never too soon to form a committee of rank and filers who track a certain issue.

Ideally, these committees draft proposals, send them around for feedback and revisions, and then bird-dog them during bargaining. It gives the bargaining team a big boost to be backed up by the specific expertise of motivated members. It also keeps member priorities front and center.

In the real world of contract negotiations, what we win depends on the power we've built. It may be that one group of members is fiercely committed to a specific proposal that's not very important to the majority. To keep this proposal from getting traded away in bargaining—and to build enough pressure that the boss will actually agree to it— this group will need to go out and talk with co-workers, explain the issue, see if they can bring others in as allies, and show that they're also willing to go to the mat for the issues that others care more about. This kind of coalition-building is only possible when bargaining is open.

What we win depends on the power we've built.

Big bargaining team. Bargaining is often treated as an arcane skill, dependent on a few highly trained specialists. It's not true! Good bargaining depends mainly on members who are committed to the collective welfare (not just their own needs), who want to listen, who are patient and steadfast, and who can work cooperatively despite many frustrations and challenges.

The team should include members from every job title, shift, worksite, or department possible. It should include young, middle-aged, and senior workers, and workers of every identity group that's present in your workplace—think race, gender, faith, language, and so on.

If your union isn't offering regular education sessions about bargaining, it should. You want a big pool of members who feel ready and able to join. Then elect your bargaining team! If that's unprecedented in your union, break precedent.

Make sure these members aren't just window dressing. It's cynical—and breeds cynicism among members—to have a big team but also a smaller team that makes all the decisions behind the curtain.

In United Teachers Los Angeles, a reform-oriented leadership expanded its bargaining team from 15 members to 90, and in the following bargaining cycle to 140. A head table, composed of a smaller group of elected leaders, coordinated the bargaining process and set direction on some priorities, but the entire bargaining team made most decisions by consensus.

It took extra time and work to make this possible—including internal education, norm-setting, and dialogue among those on the team—but the increased transparency and accountability brought an unprecedented level of legitimacy to the negotiations. Bargaining team members reported the results of each bargaining session and asked for input, which engaged many more members and ultimately led to more support for the final package.

Build team relationships. The bargaining team should schedule time together—months in advance of the start of negotiations—where members share their values, experience, ideas, and skills, and work out possible conflicts.

There will be debate, and that's wonderful. Unions should be laboratories for worker self-governance, including how to resolve real differ-

Unions should be laboratories for worker self-governance.

ences through dialogue. For example, parents of young children may have different bargaining priorities than workers nearing retirement. Conflicts over, say, paid family leave versus pensions are best worked through by bringing people together to find a mutually acceptable set of demands.

Bargaining team members should also commit to being "ambassadors" from the table to the worksite—debriefing their co-workers after each bargaining session, promoting discussion, and soliciting opinions to guide the team forward.

Open up the table. There's a wide spectrum of how far unions go in "opening up" the actual bargaining sessions. What is feasible may depend on the history, culture, power relations, fears, and practicalities of each workplace. But here are some elements to consider:

- Open sharing of all union proposals with members before they go to management
- Open sharing of management's proposals with members
- Refusing any ground rule that limits free and open reporting to members
- Comprehensive reporting after each bargaining session, with questions seeking member feedback
- Permitting rank and filers to observe bargaining sessions, in person or online
- Inviting rank and filers to speak at the table on specific topics at specific times

- Caucusing with both bargaining team and non–bargaining team members before tentatively agreeing to language
- Prohibiting sidebar negotiations (where someone from the union team meets with management privately)

Ratification. The full tentative agreement should be available to all members, not just a summary or highlights. Allow time for members to read, question, debate, and decide on the contract.

Arrange for information sessions—in person and online—that make it easy for members to participate. There should be lots of time, and a non-defensive attitude from the front of the room, for questions and discussion.

Procedures for voting should be clear, accessible, and uniform. Vote results should be fully reported, both raw numbers and percentages.

Debrief democratically. Our experiences give us insights that can guide us and those who come after us. After a contract campaign wraps up, invite all members into dialogue, not just the bargaining team members, officers, or stewards.

After a contract campaign wraps up, invite all members into dialogue.

Open the door wide by soliciting feedback, making time at union meetings, and offering special debrief sessions, both in person and online.

Don't just discuss how members feel about the settlement, though of course this is an important topic. The questions that elicit the freshest and wisest answers will be about the process—how members contributed, how they changed, what they learned, what they observed in their co-workers, and what they learned about relations of power in the workplace.

One-way newsletters

For union members trying to breathe a little life into their local, a newsletter is often the go-to solution. It can be a great way to stimulate interest, educate co-workers, increase transparency, and inspire people to get involved.

It can also be lackluster and boring. To make your union or caucus newsletter a useful organizing tool, keep some basic organizing principles in mind:

- Show members respect by treating them as partners, rather than as passive consumers.
- Inspire them with examples of what their fellow members are doing.
- Provide realistic ways for them to get more engaged.

Imagine your union has just won a good settlement on a grievance. The employee felt she had been targeted by management—verbally harassed, watched like a hawk for any small mistake, called out for violations that were typically ignored by supervisors—because of her age. How would you report on this in your newsletter?

Worst:

No coverage, out of concern for confidentiality.

Better:

This month we reached a settlement at step 3 of the grievance procedure on a case involving disparate treatment. Management agreed to remove two discipline letters from the employee's file.

Best:

This month we reached a settlement at step 3 of the grievance procedure, defending a member who felt she was being targeted because of her age. We were able to show that in fact management was treating her differently from younger workers, and got an agreement to take discipline letters out of her file.

Now we want to know if this is happening to others, and to prevent management from using this fear tactic again. Over the next two weeks, stewards will be talking with members to see if others have been targeted by management because of their age. Anything you share will be kept in confidence, unless you say it's OK to share.

Please let your steward know if this is a concern for you. [Include stewards' contact info.]

Want to learn more about how the union fights back against targeting? Come to the next "Know Your Rights Coffee Hour" at [time/date/place].

Ask yourself what information members can really use in their own worksites. Provide enough specific detail for members to understand and identify with the situations you're describing. Don't self-censor: Consider seriously when confidentiality is needed and when it's not. (Note, however, that you must have members' approval if you're going to identify them in the newsletter.)

Don't just offer information; ask questions. Offer ways for members to do something—talk to a steward, talk to co-workers, come to a meeting, send feedback or ideas.

Here's another example. Let's say a group of workers finally overcame their fear and were able to collectively confront a bullying supervisor. Amazingly enough, the supervisor was moved. How could this be covered in your newsletter?

Worst:

No coverage, for fear of management retaliation.

Better:

We're pleased to report that a group of union members finally got management to listen to them! After repeated individual complaints about difficulties with supervisor John Smith, five workers in the maintenance department got together, delivered a letter to the director of H.R., and a week later the supervisor was moved out of the department. Congratulations!

Best:

Same as above, then continuing...

Here's what's next after this victory:

> *Who knows where this bullying supervisor will land next? So far Smith hasn't been reassigned. Keep eyes and ears peeled and let your steward know if he shows up in your department. We can help you get ready to respond appropriately.*
>
> *Do you have a bully supervisor? Union members who carried out this successful effort are making themselves available to come to your department and brief you on their experience. Contact so-and-so [contact info] to set up a time to meet.*
>
> *Preparing for bargaining: With contract negotiations 18 months away, now is the perfect time to talk about contract provisions we can win to prevent supervisor bullying. We've scheduled "Bargaining Brainstorming" meetings over the next two months to generate ideas for the next contract, including how to define dignified working conditions and how to enforce them.*

Don't just report on what the president or chief negotiator has done. Highlight what rank-and-file members are thinking, saying, and doing.

Offer concrete examples of workplace action that will encourage and inspire others. Solicit, and then promote, brilliant ideas that members generate themselves.

TIPS FOR NEWSLETTER DISTRIBUTION

Find out how your co-workers like their news. Do they prefer to receive it electronically, or have a paper copy placed in their hand? Workplace cultures vary.

Don't make the mistake of assuming that just leaving a newsletter lying around, such as in the breakroom, will produce any result.

Your newsletter will have the greatest impact if it's hand-delivered to co-workers in a way that can generate a conversation: "*Hey, there's a question on page 7 that our bargaining team wants answered,*" or "*A member of your team was interviewed about the shortage of supplies. Do you see that problem too?*"

Best of all is if your newsletter connects people to other union activities. For instance, the newsletter might alert members to the topic of an upcoming meeting, and provide info that will equip them for the discussion.

Social media

It has become an article of faith that social media is essential to our organizing. But organizers who devote a lot of time to crafting and amplifying posts may find that this isn't really shifting the balance of power.

We need tools to communicate. But these tools cannot take the place of the human relationships that power effective organizing. Just as in earlier times, when typewriters and mimeograph machines, then computers and email, then cell phones and texting seemed to revolutionize our organizing methods, we start out being dazzled and may end up a bit dazed and distracted by the new technology.

If you're structuring an organizing campaign around how many posts you can place on how many platforms to generate how many hits, pause and ask yourself some questions:

- What are your goals in using social media? Who are you trying to reach, and what are you hoping people will do as a result of reading your posts? How can you assess whether you achieved the goal?
- Is your social media integrated with other kinds of outreach or education in your campaign?
- Do you find that you're using social media as a substitute for face-to-face contact (rather than a supplement to it)?

- How are you measuring the impact of this tactic? Is it helping you to build new relationships of trust or to change attitudes and opinions?
- Do you observe members going from posting to being active in other ways? Is there a plan to help people move from the relatively passive act of posting to something more engaged? Does it work?

The point here isn't to refrain from social media, but to be clear on its purpose. We can't rely on it to do the necessary work of helping co-workers become worksite organizers. That happens in relationships and as a result of collective action.

Running for union office

The quickest way to improve your union is to run for office… right?

Maybe not. This should never be off the radar for any union reformer, but it shouldn't necessarily be the default strategy.

When deciding whether to run for office, it's not enough to be disappointed with the current leadership. It's not enough to have a better program than theirs. It's not enough that your best friends are urging you to run. There are three questions to evaluate seriously:

- Do you have a plan to win?
- If you do win, are you prepared to use the office to help transform the union?
- Are you prepared to use the campaign to build a foundation for union democratization, even if you lose?

First, on winning the election: Ask yourself and your allies practical questions like: How many votes will it take? And how many phone numbers do you have on your list? For much more on the nuts and bolts of a winning campaign, consult the Labor Notes book *Running for Local Union Office*.

Don't underestimate your opponents. Incumbents who seem like do-nothings may abruptly show some initiative and organizing know-how when they discover that they're being challenged.

If you've run for office and lost, reflect on these questions:

- Was a slate of candidates put together, or did it just hang on one person? A slate is almost always a better approach.
- If there was a slate, did it reflect the diversity of the members by job title, worksite, age, race, and gender? A slate that claims to be democratic but fails to reflect the membership's profile undermines its own credibility.
- Did the campaign project what it was for, or just what it was against? Were the goals realistic or rhetorical? Did they address actual problems that members care about, or a vague "vision"? More of the former and less of the latter is a good idea.
- Did the candidates speak with members, or just give speeches? Did the candidates bring members together to talk with each other?
- Did the campaign miscalculate or discover a critical lack of knowledge in any area, such as election rules, fundraising, voter lists, or the balloting process? Which technical areas will you need to learn more about, or strategize on, before you make another attempt?

Most important, though, is taking this question seriously: What will you do if you win?

> **Consider what it will take to shift the culture of the union.**

Consider what it will take to shift the culture of the union. It's helpful to plan ahead for how you will approach the main challenges, because when you take office you will be hit with a whirlwind of things to react to. You can even start acting on some of your plans now, as part of your campaign.

If members are used to being "serviced," they may resent being exhorted to just "organize." You can arrange training for reps or staff that encourages more worksite discussion and direct problem-solving, as well as using formal grievance procedures.

If union meetings have been so sterile that no one wants to come, you can make them interesting by opening up space for discussion, popular education, and brainstorming—while still making sure to get necessary union business done. You will want to think carefully—with lots of input from others—about what to prioritize, how to communicate, and how to shift resources, so that more members become informed and engaged in union life.

If steward positions are vacant, or occupied by passive "old guard" types, you will need to identify, recruit, and train a new crop of stewards. Be prepared to respond to hurt feelings and resentments among stewards who are being displaced. Perhaps there's a continuing role for them, but they may be sharing space with others who are eager for bottom-up, trouble-making tactics.

The old ways of doing things don't just disappear because a new crop of leaders has been elected. You may find yourself trapped in these old ways, which will be frustrating to you and other members hoping for a change. So running for office is also a commitment to rework how your union operates—opening up decisions and issues that were previously closed, broadening and flattening decision-making, and relying on diverse strategies, not just grievances or lobbying, to win what members need.

Your team will continue the same kind of organizing you've been doing from the bottom up. The main difference is that now you will have more resources to put into the task. So a run for office should emerge as a logical next step out of a rank-and-file organizing group that is already growing and thriving. (If, on the other hand, your organizing inside the union hasn't been going well so far, running for—or even winning—union office isn't going to fix the problem.)

Finally, a word on productive failure. Even if your slate loses, you may have grown your support through the campaign—making new contacts, recruiting new leaders, and increasing voter participation. Sometimes incumbent leaders will even begin to adopt some of your program to stave off further challenges. This is a kind of victory too, and should be valued.

And if you've been demeaned, suffered retaliation, and taken a thrashing for having the audacity to participate in democratic elections... stay steady. Holding onto your values, even when it's really tough, is its own victory.

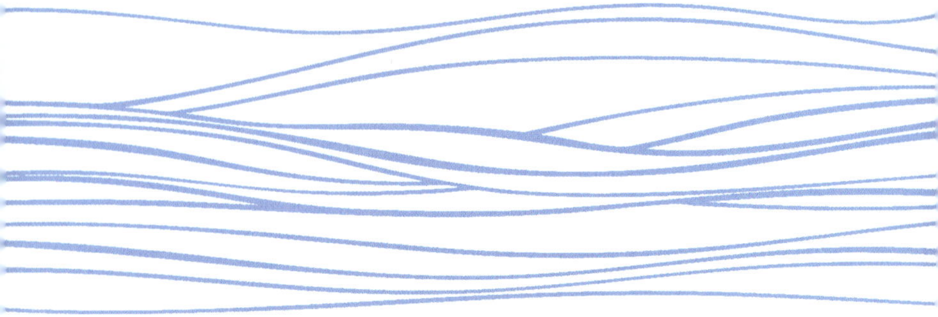

CONCLUSION: THE LONG HAUL

This struggle for democratic unions that build collective power to challenge unjust domination… it's a long haul.

Our hearts may be broken many times. But we keep going. We keep pushing and being pushed. Losing fights, and learning to master shame. Winning them, and learning to master arrogance.

We find a few comrades, or find ourselves unexpectedly embraced by a whole vast family. During those times when we are alone, we find reliable comradeship in our own insights. And we keep going, alone or together.

If we can keep going only if we get the sweet vindication of a victory, then we *won't* keep going. Our victories may be spaced very far apart, and our disappointment may surge in to fill the spaces. If so, we may drown in disappointment and lose our grip on our life preserver: a long-haul perspective.

Instead, we can fill those spaces between the victories with something else: patience. We can refuse to give up our purest intentions—and be patient as we approach our goals inch by inch.

We can ground ourselves with dignity, and offer dignity to others.

We can delight in every new insight, every new skill, and every vexing problem that we manage to face with steadiness.

We can learn day by day to calm our reactivity, our egos, and our need for control.

We can help our co-workers to become organizers, and appreciate how each person brings their own particular brand of tenacity and strength.

We can acknowledge that we will inevitably be bruised, but we can keep going and find satisfaction in growing as organizers.

We can see ourselves reaching back through history, standing firm in the present moment, and arcing confidently to the future.

The long haul calls us, and we keep going.

ABOUT THE AUTHOR

Ellen David Friedman is the board chair of Labor Notes. She has been a union organizer, strategist, and labor educator for 50 years, including 20 years at the Vermont-National Education Association and 10 years teaching, organizing, and troublemaking in Guangzhou, China. She credits Karl Marx, Paulo Freire, and the Buddha for most ideas present in this volume.

ABOUT THE ILLUSTRATOR

Fernando Martí is an Ecuadorian-born political artist, architect, writer, and housing activist, based in San Francisco (unceded Ohlone territory). His work brings together his background in liberatory urbanism and cultural organizing, his roots in rural Ecuador, and his current residence in the heart of Empire. His prints and writing can be found on *justseeds.org*.

INDEX

ABOUT LABOR NOTES

labornotes.org

Jim West/*jimwestphoto.com*

Since 1979, Labor Notes has been the voice of activists putting the *movement* back in the labor movement. We're a network of thousands of rank-and-file members and union leaders who believe that an injury to one is an injury to all. Through our magazine, website, books, and events, we encourage connections between workers in different unions, industries, and countries to strengthen the movement from the bottom up.

Labor Notes can become your lifeline and home base. Visit *labornotes.org* to learn more and join our free weekly email list. If you enjoyed this book and find our work valuable, consider becoming a monthly donor, which comes with a cool T-shirt.

EVENTS

One-day **Troublemakers Schools** build skills and solidarity among members of different unions. Our **online workshops** include organizing basics, steward tips, and Ellen David Friedman's What to Do When Your Union Breaks Your Heart. And every two years, thousands of people gather for a big dose of inspiration at the **Labor Notes Conference**. See what's coming up at *labornotes.org/events*

SUBSCRIBE TO LABOR NOTES

labornotes.org/subscribe

Our monthly magazine is packed with news you won't find anywhere else, including honest analysis of labor's latest victories and defeats, often written by the people on the front lines. Use it to discover new tactics, start conversations on union strategy, and link up to the inspiration and energy of a wider labor movement.

We report with a rank-and-file audience in mind, getting details of not just what workers are fighting for but also *how* they're doing it, much like the stories in this book. Every issue features a "Steward's Corner" full of advice from experts and stories from organizers.

It's $30 for one year (11 issues), to any U.S. address.

BUNDLE SUBSCRIPTION

labornotes.org/bundle

Want to share *Labor Notes* with your co-workers, shop stewards, or executive board? Many individuals, caucuses, and local unions receive a bundle of five to 200 copies of every new issue, to distribute at meetings or hand around on the job.

Bundle prices start at $50 per year for five copies per month, to any U.S. address.

SECRETS OF A SUCCESSFUL ORGANIZER

labornotes.org/secrets

Are there problems where you work? Maybe your pay is too low, conditions are unsafe, or your boss has it in for someone you work with... and you're ready to do something about it.

This book will show you how to fight back where you work and win. You'll learn how to identify the key issues in your workplace, build campaigns to tackle them, anticipate management's tricks and traps, and inspire your co-workers to stand together despite their fears.

We've distilled generations of organizing know-how into 47 easily accessible secrets. Put them all together and you've got a step-by-step guide to building power on the job.

This book is also available in Spanish from Labor Notes. Activists around the world have translated it into Chinese (simplified and traditional), Danish, German, Japanese, Quebecois French, and Swedish.

Also available: A trainer's guide designed as a companion to this book.

$15, bulk discounts available

MORE FROM LABOR NOTES

Find more Labor Notes books, including *How to Jump-Start Your Union*, *The Legal Rights of Union Stewards*, *Democracy Is Power*, and *Running for Local Union Office*, plus the Troublemakers Union T-shirt, at *labornotes.org/store*.

PM Press is an independent, radical publisher of books and media to educate, entertain, and inspire. Founded in 2007 by a small group of people with decades of publishing, media, and organizing experience, PM Press amplifies the voices of radical authors, artists, and activists. Our aim is to deliver bold political ideas and vital stories to all walks of life and arm the dreamers to demand the impossible. We have sold millions of copies of our books, most often one at a time, face to face. We're old enough to know what we're doing and young enough to know what's at stake. Join us to create a better world.

PM Press
PO Box 23912
Oakland CA 94623
510-703-0327
www.pmpress.org

PM Press in Europe
europe@pmpress.org
www.pmpress.org.uk

FRIENDS OF PM

These are indisputably momentous times—the financial system is melting down globally and the Empire is stumbling. Now more than ever there is a vital need for radical ideas.

In the many years since its founding—and on a mere shoestring—PM Press has risen to the formidable challenge of publishing and distributing knowledge and entertainment for the struggles ahead. With hundreds of releases to date, we have published an impressive and stimulating array of literature, art, music, politics, and culture. Using every available medium, we've succeeded in connecting those hungry for ideas and information to those putting them into practice.

Friends of PM allows you to directly help impact, amplify, and revitalize the discourse and actions of radical writers, filmmakers, and artists. It provides us with a stable foundation from which we can build upon our early successes and provides a much-needed subsidy for the materials that can't necessarily pay their own way. You can help make that happen—and receive every new title automatically delivered to your door once a month—by joining as a Friend of PM Press. And, we'll throw in a free T-shirt when you sign up.

Here are your options:

- **$30 a month** Get all books and pamphlets plus 50% discount on all webstore purchases
- **$40 a month** Get all PM Press releases (including CDs and DVDs) plus 50% discount on all webstore purchases
- **$100 a month** Superstar—Everything plus PM merchandise, free downloads, and 50% discount on all webstore purchases

For those who can't afford $30 or more a month, we have **Sustainer Rates** at $15, $10, and $5. Sustainers get a free PM Press T-shirt and a 50% discount on all purchases from our website.

Your Visa or Mastercard will be billed once a month, until you tell us to stop. Or until our efforts succeed in bringing the revolution around. Or the financial meltdown of Capital makes plastic redundant. Whichever comes first.

Labor Power and Strategy

John Womack Jr.
Edited by Peter Olney and Glenn Perušek

ISBN: 978-1-62963-974-1 • $16.95 • 208 pages

In this sleek, practical, pocket inspiration, Womack lays out a timely plan for identifying chokepoints and taking advantage of supply chain issues in order to seize and build labor power and solidarity. In interviews by Peter Olney of the International Longshore and Warehouse Union, Womack's lively, illuminating thoughts are built upon by ten labor organizers and educators, whose responses create a rich dialogue and open a space for joyful, achievable change. With inspiring stories of triumph, this back-pocket primer is an instant classic.

Contributors include: Gene Bruskin, Carey Dall, Dan DiMaggio, Katy Fox-Hodess, Bill Fletcher Jr., Jane McAlevey, Jack Metzgar, Joel Ochoa, Melissa Shetler, and Rand Wilson.

What the Boss Doesn't Want Us to Know: Discovering Power and Winning Campaigns

Tom Juravich, Olivia Geho, and Andrew Gorry

ISBN: 9798887441023 • $17.95 • 200 pages

After the labor movement faded away in the lives of most Americans, organizing is back!

What the Boss Doesn't Want Us to Know is for more than just professional researchers and campaigners. This book offers up a radical new practice for investigating employers. The authors propose a member-based, democratic approach to corporate research that will train an army of rank-and-file researchers to investigate and beat the firms that control so much of our lives. This approach has already been successfully utilized with NewsGuild of New York at the *New York Times*, Reuters, Gannett, the United Food and Commercial Workers at Tyson Foods, workers at Google (the Alphabet Workers Union), Apple retail workers, the Association of Flight Attendants at Delta Air Lines, and Trader Joe's United. The lessons contained in this book hold great promise to supercharge the new organizing wave currently sweeping across America.